V. KARPINSKY

THE SOCIAL AND STATE STRUCTURE OF THE U.S.S.R.

V. KARPINSKY

THE SOCIAL AND STATE STRUCTURE OF THE U.S.S.R.

GREENWOOD PRESS, PUBLISHERS
WESTPORT, CONNECTICUT

Originally published in 1948
by the Foreign Languages Publishing House, Moscow

Reprinted from an original copy in the collections
of the University of Illinois Library

First Greenwood Reprinting 1970

Library of Congress Catalogue Card Number 79-98775

SBN 8371-3116-2

Printed in the United States of America

CONTENTS

	Page
THE STALIN CONSTITUTION	9

CHAPTER I

SOVIET SOCIALIST SOCIETY 13

Socialism in the Everyday Life of the People 13
Socialist Property 16
Two Forms of Socialist Property 19
Socialist, Planned Economy 24
The Superiority of Socialist, Planned Economy Over Capitalist Economy 25
Work in Soviet Socialist Society 29
The Moral and Political Unity of Soviet Society. . . . 31

CHAPTER II

THE SOVIET SOCIALIST STATE 34

The Soviets 34
The Soviet Republic 36
The Primary and Fundamental Basis of the Soviet State 37
Guidance of Soviet Society by the State 41
The Superiority of the Soviet State Over the Capitalist States 45

CHAPTER III

THE STATE STRUCTURE OF THE UNION OF SOVIET SOCIALIST REPUBLICS 48

The Status of the Peoples Composing the Soviet Union 48
What Is the Soviet Union? 50
What Is a Union Republic? 54

	Page
What Is an Autonomous Republic?	59
What Is an Autonomous Region?	63
What Is a National Area?	65
The Friendship of the Soviet Peoples Is Indestructible	68

CHAPTER IV

THE HIGHER ORGANS OF STATE POWER AND OF STATE ADMINISTRATION OF THE U.S.S.R. 71

How the Organs of State Power Are Formed in Our Country	71
Those Whom the People Have Entrusted with Supreme Power in the Country	80
The Supreme Soviet of the U.S.S.R.	85
The Presidium of the Supreme Soviet of the U.S.S.R.	90
The Council of Ministers of the U.S.S.R.	94

CHAPTER V

THE COURTS AND THE PROCURATOR'S OFFICE 100

The Old Landlord-Bourgeois Courts	100
The Soviet Courts and Their Functions	102
Soviet Judicial Organs	104
The Only Genuine People's Court in the World	106
The Soviet Procurator's Office	108

CHAPTER VI

THE FUNDAMENTAL RIGHTS OF SOVIET CITIZENS   113

Citizens of the Soviet Union	113
The Right to Work	114
The Right to Rest and Leisure	119
The Right to Material Security	124
The Right to Education	127
The Equality of Men and Women	130
The Equality of Citizens of All Nationalities and Races	134
Freedom of Conscience	138
Political Liberties	140

CHAPTER VII

THE FUNDAMENTAL DUTIES OF SOVIET CITIZENS 145

    On Rights and Duties 145
    To Abide by the Stalin Constitution, to Observe the
        Soviet Laws 147
    To Maintain Labour Discipline 148
    Honestly to Perform Public Duties 153
    To Respect the Rules of Socialist Intercourse 156
    To Safeguard and Fortify Public, Socialist Property . . 160
    An Honourable Duty of Soviet Citizens 164
    The Sacred Duty of Every Soviet Citizen 169

CHAPTER VIII

THE LEADING AND DIRECTING FORCE OF THE SOVIET
UNION . . , ... 175

THE STALIN CONSTITUTION

THE CONSTITUTION of a country is its fundamental law. The present Constitution of the U.S.S.R. was adopted at the Extraordinary Eighth Congress of Soviets of the U.S.S.R. on December 5, 1936. It has been popularly named the *Stalin Constitution* after its author, Comrade Stalin.

The Stalin Constitution concisely sets forth the fundamental principles of the new, socialist system of society and of the new, Soviet structure of our multinational state. Ours is the first country in the history of mankind to have established such a system, such a structure of society. Herein lies the supreme, historic importance of the Stalin Constitution.

The Soviet Constitution registers and gives legislative embodiment to what has already been actually achieved.

The first Soviet Constitution, drawn up under the guidance of V. I. Lenin and J. V. Stalin, was adopted by the Fifth All-Russian Congress of Soviets on July 10, 1918. What did it record and what did it enact into law?

It speaks of the transfer of all state power to the Soviets, of equal rights possessed by all peoples inhabiting our country, of the transfer of all land, its natural deposits and its forests and waters to the whole of the people as their common property; it speaks of the transfer of the banks to the state of the workers and peasants, of workers' control over industrial, trading and agricultural enterprises, and of the organization of central and local organs of Soviet power.

But the Constitution of 1918 says nothing about recording the establishment of a socialist system in our country. Too little time had elapsed since the conquest of power to enable the whole country to be reconstructed and placed on a socialist footing. In his report to the Fifth All-Russian Congress of Soviets, Lenin said:

"... we do not yet know of a Socialism that can be put into paragraphs of law."

In 1922 the Union of Soviet Socialist Republics was formed. A new Constitution, the first Constitution of the U.S.S.R., was drawn up under the guidance of V. I. Lenin and J. V. Stalin, and was adopted on January 31, 1924 by the Second All-Union Congress of Soviets. It ordained and recorded the formation of a federal Soviet state, the formation of new, all-Union organs of state power and state administration.

But in this Constitution too you will find nothing concerning the embodiment of a socialist system. At that time Socialism was still in the making.

The first and second Stalin Five-Year Plans (1928-1937) radically altered the whole economy of our country. During these years a new, socialist industry was created in the U.S.S.R., the collective-farm system emerged victorious, and the socialist ownership of the means of production was established throughout the national economy as the basis of Soviet society. During this period the relation of class forces in our country changed completely: all exploiting classes were abolished and the exploitation of man by man eliminated. The working class, the peasantry and the intelligentsia were utterly transformed. The friendship and fraternal co-operation between the peoples of the Soviet Union gained strength. The victory of Socialism in the U.S.S.R. made possible the further democratization of the Soviet electoral system.

All these great changes in the life of our country are reflected in the Stalin Constitution. It briefly records the facts denoting the complete liberation of the working people of the U.S.S.R. from capitalist bondage, the victory of Socialism in the Soviet Union and its fully developed and strictly consistent democracy (government of and by the people).

All organs of state power and state administration in our country are formed in accordance with the Constitution. The Constitution is the basis upon which all Soviet bodies and institutions function and all Soviet laws are adopted. And it is the Constitution which establishes the principal rights and duties of Soviet citizens.

Speaking on the significance of our Constitution, Comrade Stalin said:

"After the path of struggle and privation that has been traversed, it is pleasant and joyful to have our Constitution, which treats of the fruits of our victories. It is pleasant and joyful to know what our people fought for and how they achieved this victory of world-wide historical importance. It is pleasant and joyful to know that the blood our people shed so plentifully was not shed in vain, that it has produced results. This arms our working class, our peasantry, our working intelligentsia spiritually. It impels them forward and rouses a sense of legitimate pride. It increases confidence in our strength and mobilizes us for fresh struggles for the achievement of new victories of Communism."

The international significance which attaches to our Constitution is also great. On acquainting themselves with its contents, the labouring masses abroad come to regard it as the incarnation of all their long-cherished hopes and expectations, and derive from it the strength to fight for their own emancipation.

Every Soviet citizen ought to know the Stalin Constitution, as it is the fundamental law of his country and a great historical document attesting to the victory of Socialism and genuine democracy in the Soviet Union, as it is the banner of liberation and of friendship among the peoples.

CHAPTER I

SOVIET SOCIALIST SOCIETY

SOCIALISM IN THE EVERYDAY LIFE OF THE PEOPLE

THERE WAS a time when Socialism was merely a theory, a doctrine, and the question of whether it could be put into practice was much disputed. Now Socialism has already been built in the U.S.S.R., Socialism has become part and parcel of the everyday life of the peoples of the Soviet Union.

Socialism in practice means the absence of exploitation and oppression of man by man, the abolition of unemployment and destitution, uninterrupted progress in the welfare and culture of the popular masses. Socialism in practice implies the new relations that have taken shape in our society, relations of co-operation and mutual assistance among people free from exploitation. Socialism in practice means the proud consciousness of the fact that you work for yourself and for a society composed of work-people like yourself, that you are a full-fledged member of this society, that you are master of your country and of all its wealth.

Comrade Stalin has said:

"Our mills and factories are being run without capitalists. The work is directed by men and women of the people. That is what we call Socialism in practice. In our fields the tillers of the land work without landlords and without kulaks. The work is directed by men and women of the people. This is what we call Socialism in daily life, this is what we call a free, socialist life."

There is no difficulty in corroborating Stalin's words with facts culled from life. There is, for instance, the Korobov family, famous throughout the Soviet Union. The father, I. G. Korobov, born in 1882, is an old blast-furnace man, a trade that has run in the family for generations. When a boy he attended elementary school for two winter seasons and then got a job hauling ore. Thanks to his resourcefulness and perseverance he managed to be promoted to foreman, a rare occurrence in the old days. Since 1918 he has been head foreman in the blast-furnace department at the Kirov Plant in Makeyevka.

In 1937 the people elected I. G. Korobov a Deputy to the Supreme Soviet of the Ukrainian Soviet Socialist Republic, and in 1946 a Deputy to the Supreme Soviet of the U.S.S.R.

Korobov's three sons, graduates of Soviet universities, now hold responsible positions. Nikolai Korobov is the director of the State Institute for the Designing of Metallurgical Plants. Pavel Korobov is Vice-Minister of the Iron and Steel Industry. In 1937 he was elected Deputy to the Supreme Soviet of the U.S.S.R. and re-elected in 1946. The third son, Ilya, is the director of the huge Petrovsky Steel Mill in the Ukraine.

After one of the metallurgists' conferences in Moscow, Comrade Stalin, at a reception held in the Kremlin, pronounced a toast in honour of the old and new blast-furnace department workers, and in honour of the whole Korobov family. Then, turning to Korobov senior, he said in his friendly way:

"Well done! Thanks for raising such a family."

"It's all right saying 'well done,'" replied Korobov, "but if it hadn't been for the Soviet system there would have been nothing well done about me!"

The leaders of our industry stem from the working class and the peasantry, and also from the intelligentsia.

The same applies to agriculture.

Let us illustrate the point with the Timiryazev Collective Farm [kolkhoz], in Gorodets District, Gorky Region. It is a small town in itself, with substantial tile-covered buildings, an electric power station and water works, a club, school, hospital, maternity home, kindergartens and nurseries, and a diversity of cultural establishments. A huge stretch of land consisting of 3,189 hectares has been assigned to this *kolkhoz* by government deed for its perpetual use. The collective farm has five departments: a dairy, a hog-raising, a sheep-raising and a poultry farm, and a stud farm breeding pedigree race horses. In addition the collective farm owns a number of subsidiary enterprises: a windmill, a steam mill. a creamery, a brickkiln and tilery, a pottery, a shoe and felt-boot shop, a woodworking shop and an apiary.

This complex, handsomely-provided public establishment is directed by a neighbourhood peasant named I. A. Emelyanov, who was born in 1901 in the village of Medvedkovo. He organized this collective farm in 1930, became its chairman and has been regularly re-elected to this post ever since. In 1930, too, he was admitted to the Communist Party.

Examples like this can be cited without end. They all confirm the fact that in the Soviet Union the working people themselves carry on their socialist economy, and carry on without capitalists and without landlords; that in the Soviet Union a just, socialist system of society, that system for which thousands of the foremost people in our country have laid down their lives, has actually been realized under the leadership of the Bolshevik Party.

Let us examine now the structure of socialist society.

SOCIALIST PROPERTY

On May Day of 1919, V. I. Lenin, speaking in the Red Square in Moscow, told the people:

"Our grandchildren will regard the documents and memorials of the epoch of the capitalist system as curiosities. It will be difficult for them to picture to themselves how the trade in articles of prime necessity could be in private hands, how the factories and works could belong to individual persons, how one man could exploit another, how there could be people who did not work."

And indeed it is very difficult for our youth, born and bred under Soviet rule, to imagine the system of society that prevailed in tsarist Russia, where the factories and mills, the instruments and means of production, the fields, meadows and mountains, the forests and waters were the *private property* of the idle rich, while the millions of workers and poor peasants eked out a starvation existence, as they had to sell their labour-power to the capitalists, the landlords and the kulaks.

Here, for instance, we have before us the pay-book of Yegor Vlasov, a worker of the Putilov Plant. The book states that Vlasov was getting a wage of 50 kopeks a day, making 6 rubles and 50 kopeks a fortnight. From this sum there was deducted 5 rubles 43 kopeks for food, bought on credit at the factory store, and 13 kopeks for the church, *94 kopeks* being paid to him in cash.

Thus we see that a worker drudging for a capitalist from early morning till late in the day used to receive (besides his "food") less than 2 rubles a month with which to satisfy all his other needs.

The following case occurred at the Semyannikov Factory in St. Petersburg. A worker named Yefim Lakhnov was riveting a boiler that was suspended from the chain of a jib crane. The worker noticed that the chain was giving and went to tell the shop superintendent. The latter only shouted at him to get on with the job. Before an hour went by the boiler came down with a terrible crash—the defective chain had snapped. The workers rushed to the scene but were too late to do anything for their comrade. He had been crushed to death. The superintendent, who was standing nearby, smoking, remarked to the engineer:

"What a pity, there's a dent in the boiler now!"

The boiler, you see, cost its owner money, whereas the life of his worker cost him nothing. Any number of other workers were ready to take the dead man's place.

The mass of the peasants, too, led a very hard life. The landlords had seized vast stretches of land. The less than 30,000 large landed proprietors owned as much land as the 10,000,000 poor peasants. For example, in the village of Sanskoye, Province of Ryazan, the landlord Podlazov alone had twice as much land as 918 of the local peasant households. The peasants had to work for a pittance for the landlord, lease land from him, become sharecroppers on his estate, his share, unearned, being half the crop.

The old workers and peasants experienced all the horrors of the bourgeois and landlord system based on private property. But the Soviet youth has never set eye on capitalists or landlords. From childhood it has been accustomed to an entirely different system, a system based on *socialist property*.

What is meant by socialist property?

According to the Stalin Constitution, the land, its mineral wealth, waters, forests, mines, mills, factories, state farms, machine and tractor stations, banks, rail, water and air transport, communications (post, telegraph, telephone, radio), municipal enterprises and the bulk of the dwelling houses in the cities are all *state, socialist property, that is, belong to the whole people.*

Thus the bulk and principal part of all means of production in our country are state, socialist property.

The buildings and establishments of the collective farms and co-operative organizations, including equipment and machinery, their working cattle and their livestock departments, constitute *co-operative and collective-farm socialist property.*

The great importance of co-operative and collective-farm socialist property appears from the fact that the vast majority of peasant farms in our country have been united into collective farms. In 1940 almost 97 per cent of the total number of farm households belonged to collective farms.

Under Soviet law individual peasants and handicraftsmen may each have a small private establishment of their own on condition that it is operated by their own labour only, that is, without exploiting the labour of others.

Soviet law likewise protects the personal property right of all citizens in their incomes and savings from work, in their dwelling houses, their subsidiary home enterprises, their household goods and their articles of personal use and convenience. Soviet law also safeguards the right of inheritance of personal property.

Socialist economy based on socialist property, that is, property belonging to the state or to co-operatives and collective farms, holds the dominant position in our country. It is of decisive importance in the life of the people and is the principal source of the well-being of Soviet citizens.

Every one of us should clearly realize the vast importance of socialist property for the working people, for our country, for our state.

Why can nobody in our country force any one to work for him?

For the simple reason that the land, the instruments and other means of production in our country constitute *socialist* and not private property.

Why is there no unemployment or pauperism in our country?

Because in our country the land, mills, factories, mines, banks, transport and communications, printing presses, schools, libraries, theatres, cinemas, hospitals, sanatoria and so forth are socialist property. They all serve the working people, are there for their benefit, and are not a means of enriching private proprietors, as is the case in capitalist countries.

Why was our formerly backward country transformed, in an unprecedentedly short period of time, into one of the strongest powers in the world, a power capable of defending its liberty and upholding its independence in the struggle against fascist Germany and imperialist Japan?

Because its system of socialist ownership served as the basis on which we set up a powerful industry and a highly productive agriculture operated on the largest scale in the world, and on which we provided excellent equipment and ample supplies for the Red Army.

Socialist ownership is the *foundation of our entire social system*. And herein lies its strength, this constitutes the radical difference between it and the capitalist system, which is based on the private ownership of the instruments and means of production.

TWO FORMS OF SOCIALIST PROPERTY

As we have seen, the Stalin Constitution speaks of two forms of socialist property: state property, and co-operative and collective-farm property. Why do we have two and not one form of socialist property?

The old industrial and large-scale agricultural enterprises were taken away from the capitalists and landlords and made the property of the Soviet state. In the periods covered by the Stalin Five-Year Plans a very great number of new factories and mills, coal and ore mines, oil wells and large electric power stations have been built in our country, while in agriculture many state farms and machine and tractor stations have been set up. All these enterprises have been established by using the human and material resources of the Soviet state. The very land on which they are located belongs to the state. It is therefore quite comprehensible that all these enterprises and their entire output are *state property*, that is, *belong to the whole people*.

Now take the collective farms with all their fields and departments, their implements of production and their buildings and establishments. How did they originate? Each collective farm was built up from the resources of its members, the peasants who formed it, the state supplying aid and leadership. Each was formed by the voluntary pooling of the principal means of production, the labour-power and the land allotments of the constituent peasant families in order to constitute a single collective economy, the *kolkhoz*, or collective farm. Clearly, all the equipment of the collective farm and all its output are the *common property of the peasants* who organized the collective farm. Only the land on which the collective farm is situated is state property. But it is secured to the collective farm by a special deed for its gratuitous use in perpetuity.

Hence the existence in our country of two forms of socialist property is of historical origin. It is intimately connected with the different origins of our socialist enterprises: the state enterprises, on the one hand, and the co-operative and collective-farm enterprises, on the other.

There are also other differences between state enterprises and co-operative and collective-farm enterprises.

Who owns the state enterprise? The *Soviet state*. Soviet authorities appoint the director to manage the enterprise. The workers and other employees of the enterprise are paid by the state in accordance with the quantity and quality of the work each performs.

And who owns the collective farm? The *peasants* who are its members own it *collectively*. Its affairs are managed by the general meeting of its members, and between meetings by the collective-farm management, elected by the general meeting.

The collective farm must meet certain obligations to the state: pay its monetary taxes, deliver (that is, sell at a fixed price) to the state such part of its produce as is prescribed by law. The collective farm must pay, in kind and in money, to the state-owned machine and tractor station for work done. But only a small part of the collective-farm's income goes in discharge of these obligations. All the rest of the collective income of the peasants forming the *kolkhoz* is disposed of by them collectively at their discretion, as is set forth in the Agricultural Artel Rules.*

The collective farmers do not receive any wages from the state, as do the workers of a factory or state farm (an agricultural enterprise owned and operated by the state). The collective farmers are paid for their work out of the income of their collective farm at the end of the agricultural year, at which time this income is determined. Payment is made both

---

* *Agricultural Artel Rules.* The Rules of the Agricultural Artel (*kolkhoz*—collective farm), adopted by the general meeting of collective farmers, regulate the activities of the collective farm (problems of organization of labour, payment of labour of collective farmers, discipline, etc.).

in money and in kind (produce) on the basis of "labour days"* worked, which *corresponds to the quantity and quality of work each collective-farm member contributed to the collective enterprise.*

In addition to his income from the common, collective-farm enterprise, each collective farmer derives an income from the farming he does privately on his small subsidiary plot of land attached, under the Constitution, to his dwelling (his private cattle, truck garden, orchard, etc.). Collective farms as such and their members individually may freely sell their surplus produce on the market.

Such are the differences between our state and our co-operative and collective-farm enterprises. These differences are very important. However, there is no fundamental difference between the two forms of enterprises in our country. The underlying principles which govern both are the same. What are these principles?

The means of production in both categories of enterprises are public, and not private, property. In state enterprises they belong to the whole people, that is, to the whole of society; in co-operative and collective-farm enterprises they belong to separate public organizations. But in either case the means of production in our country are *public, socialist property.*

Whether the enterprise in question is state-owned or owned by a co-operative society or collective farm, people working in it are engaged in *public*, not private, *economy*. Whether the enterprise in question belongs to the whole people, that is, to the whole of society, or to a single public organization, the people engaged in it are paid for their work

---

* *Labour day*—unit employed in calculating work done by collective farmers. Determines both amount and quality of work to be done in one day. A collective farmer may earn more than one "labour day" in the course of a day's actual work.

according to the general *socialist* principle recorded in the Stalin Constitution:

"From each according to his ability, to each according to his work."

Both kinds of enterprises are conducted in accordance with a single national-economic plan in the interests of the working people, of Soviet society, of the Soviet state.

Thus, although different in form, our state and our co-operative and collective-farm enterprises are *identical in their socialist essence*. In neither of these two kinds of enterprises is the exploitation of man by man possible.

The state socialist enterprises serve as models of large-scale machine-operated socialist economic units for the collective farms and co-operatives.

The co-operative and collective-farm socialist enterprises were the medium through which the peasants came to Socialism. The collective farms are schools of practical experience in which tens of millions of Soviet peasants have learnt socialist farming and are learning how to perfect and develop it further.

The fact that here there is no private ownership of the means of production and no exploitation of man by man draws a fundamental line of distinction between our socialist society and capitalist society, which is based on the exploitation of the vast majority of society, the labouring masses, by an insignificant minority of idlers.

All our state and all our co-operative and collective-farm enterprises, taken together, our socialist economy in its entirety, constitute the monolithic *economic foundation of Soviet socialist society*.

SOCIALIST, PLANNED ECONOMY

Let us examine more closely how our enterprises work. Take, for instance, the cotton-growing collective farms of the Soviet Republics in Central Asia. They yield mountains of snow-white fibre. The cotton goes to our state-owned cotton mills, where it is spun and woven into millions of metres of cloth. In the needle-trades shops these textiles are turned into cotton goods for general consumption.

The grain-growing collective farms provide the country with cereals—bread for the workers and the Soviet Army.

On the other hand, the factories and mills produce machines, chemical fertilizers, kerosene, salt, sugar, textile goods, footwear, household utensils, books, newspapers, bicycles, radios and other manufactured goods.

As we see, the various branches of our national economy and their separate enterprises are closely interlocked and in their entirety constitute a *unified socialist national economy*. Each separate enterprise is only a small cog in the vast machinery of our national economy.

Naturally, none of our enterprises can do as it pleases, can produce what and as it sees fit. Every enterprise must do its share of the work that the whole country stands in need of; or, putting it differently, each enterprise must work according to a previously drawn-up plan, and this plan must be part of the *unified national-economic plan.*

The national-economic plan is drawn up by the State Planning Commission (Gosplan) of the U.S.S.R. Every Soviet Republic, Territory, Region, Area and District has its planning commission.

A plan for the development of the national economy is prepared in our country for each year and for entire five-year periods. Calculations are made, for a year or five years in advance, of what articles each branch of the national economy is to produce and in what quantities, what materials it will need for this purpose and in what quantities, with what machines and other equipment it must be provided and in what quantities, how much labour productivity can and must be raised and production costs lowered, what new establishments must be built, how many workers must be trained and what skills they must possess, etc. On the basis of these constituent plans a specific plan is drawn up for each individual enterprise.

Thus our entire national economy operates according to a unified national-economic plan, under a single directing centre, with the aim of increasing social wealth, of steadily improving the material and cultural well-being of the working people, of strengthening the independence of our country and enhancing its defensive capacity.

This is one of the fundamental differences between our socialist society and capitalist society, where each proprietor conducts his business exclusively in his own interest, for the purpose of making profit.

THE SUPERIORITY OF SOCIALIST, PLANNED ECONOMY OVER CAPITALIST ECONOMY

Let us see what socialist, planned economy means for the people and why it is superior to capitalist economy.

In our country, thanks to the introduction of the public, socialist ownership of the means of production, everyone is assured of work in either a state enterprise or a co-operative or collective-farm enterprise. In the Soviet Union people work for themselves and not for exploiters.

In the capitalist countries the situation is entirely different. There the choicest land, the factories and mills and other means of production belong to the capitalists and landlords. The wealth of the nation is concentrated in the hands of a small number of big proprietors. For instance, in the United States there is a small group of sixty people, the biggest capitalists, each one of whom owns over a billion dollars. Yet the vast majority of the population of this extremely rich country is very badly off. In 1944 the University of California estimated that a family of four needed a minimun of about 3,000 dollars a year to make ends meet, and that 70 per cent of American families had incomes below that figure. By the middle of 1947 staple foods had more than doubled in price. President Truman declared that the United States was short of five million dwelling houses and that ten and a half million occupied houses were unfit for human habitation. In the same country, during 1920-1938 alone, over 31 million farmers were unable to make a living and fled to the cities. During the same period almost 23 million unemployed left the cities to work on the farms.

In the capitalist countries the industrial and agricultural workers as well as the poor farmers and peasants are compelled, in order to keep the wolf from the door, to hire themselves out to the wealthy, receiving wretched pay for their work. The capitalists, landlords and prosperous farmers steadily grow richer by letting others work for them, while all those who have to toil grow poorer and poorer. In bourgeois countries there are always millions of unemployed.

But this is not all. In the capitalist countries there is no planning of the national economy. Each owner of an establishment is concerned only about getting as much profit out of it as he can. But the capitalists do not give a thought to the economy of the country as a whole, nor to the improvement of the material conditions of the working people. On the contrary, they resort to every method to cut wages in order that their profits may increase.

Yet the labouring masses make up the bulk of the people buying consumer goods. Now since they are kept in poverty and their jobs are insecure, their purchasing power is very limited and keeps falling constantly. Therefore it is inevitable in capitalist countries that from time to time there should be an "overproduction" of goods. Merchandise lies unsold on the shelves and in the warehouses, prices fall, factories and mills shut their doors, crop areas are cut down and millions of workers are thrown on the street. An economic crisis sets in.

In order to bring prices back to their former levels and save their profits, the capitalists destroy their "surplus" goods. They burn them, let them rot in the ground or dump them into the ocean. But even this does not help. The piles of merchandise they have stacked up are absorbed only gradually, and economic revival is very slow.

Such economic crises in capitalist countries recur every twelve, ten, or eight years and even more often. At a time of economic crisis unemployment rises until it reaches a total of tens of millions of people. During the world crisis of 1929-1933, for instance, about thirty million people were out of work.

Economic crises are a senseless waste of the means of production and of labour-power; they retard the development of the productive forces in the capitalist countries.

In socialist society there are no economic crises and there can be none. Here the means of production are public, socialist property and serve to satisfy the needs of the population. They cannot possibly be used for the exploitation of man by man. Our whole economy works according to a plan, in the interests of the whole of society, of all who work by hand or brain. The material security of the toiling masses steadily increases under Socialism, as does the demand for all kinds of articles of general consumption.

This calls for an uninterrupted expansion of production, the building of more and more new enterprises, the enlargement of crop areas, etc. Closing down factories and mills is utterly inconceivable in our country.

Socialist, planned economy based on public ownership ensures a constant growth of the productive forces of society. In no capitalist country does the national economy develop as rapidly as in the Soviet Union. The average annual increase in industrial production for the period 1917-1936 was 1 per cent in the United States, and less than 1 per cent in England. But in the U.S.S.R. the increase averaged 20 per cent a year during the first two Stalin Five-Year Plan periods (1928-1937).

To quote Comrade Stalin:

"It must be admitted that a system of economy which does not know what to do with its 'surplus' output, and can only burn it at a time when the masses are in the grip of want and unemployment, hunger and misery—such a system of economy signs its own death warrant.

"... The Soviet system of economy possesses *advantages* that not a single bourgeois state can dare to dream of...."

These advantages made themselves particularly felt during the Patriotic War, when the Soviet Union was compelled to fight against one of the strongest military powers—fascist Germany—and its allies. Moreover Germany could rely on the economic resources and the manpower of almost the whole of Western Europe that it had conquered. Nevertheless the Soviet Union emerged victorious from this most grievous of wars. Why?

Comrade Stalin explains this as follows:

"... the economic basis of the Soviet state is immeasurably more virile than the economies of the enemy countries have proved to be...."

Socialist, planned economy, based on public, socialist property, is one of the principal sources of the strength and might of the Soviet Union.

WORK IN SOVIET SOCIALIST SOCIETY

In old Russia work was the *private* affair of those who were compelled to engage in it. If you had a job you bent your back for the capitalist or landlord. If you were out of a job, that was your hard luck and nobody worried whether you starved to death or not. Work was a burdensome duty in the eyes of the toiling masses, and a despised occupation in the eyes of the bourgeoisie.

A person's station in life and in society depended on whether he was rich or poor, on how many wage-slaves he had in his employ, on who his parents were, etc. Wealthy idlers, who had appropriated the fruits of the work of others, were held in high esteem.

This is still how matters stand in all capitalist countries.

In our country a man's position in society does not depend on the amount of property he owns, his race or nationality or the post he occupies. Whoever one may be, his position in society is determined solely by his personal work and his personal ability.

In the Soviet Union work is a matter of *public* concern. Here is what Comrade Stalin said on the position of the working people in socialist society:

"Here the working man is held in esteem.... Here... the man who works feels himself a free citizen of his country, a public figure, in a way. And if he works well and gives society his best—he is a hero of labour, and is covered with glory."

What other country is there in which a person can become a hero, is held in honour and esteem, for success in the sphere of ordinary physical or mental work?

It is only in our socialist country that coal-cutters, forgemen, shoe operators, weavers, railwaymen, grain-growers, milkmaids, shepherds, teachers, flyers, physicians, scientists—people in all walks of life—become distinguished personages decorated by the state for meritorious work.

The position of honour assigned to labour in socialist society led to a fundamental change in the old-fashioned view held by workfolk with regard to work, the view that it was a burdensome duty. As early as 1930 Comrade Stalin pointed out that work is "a matter of *honour,* a matter of *glory,* a matter of *valour* and *heroism.*"

Only under our system of society was it possible for socialist emulation—a friendly contest for the speediest and best fulfilment and over-fulfilment of assigned tasks—to arise and become so widespread among the working people. Only in our country was it possible for the Stakhanov movement, which Comrade Stalin called the most virile and irresistible movement of our time, to attain such wide development in all branches of economy.

The Stalin Constitution declares that work is a *matter of honour and a duty* for every able-bodied citizen.

Socialist society demands that each able-bodied person work honestly, that his work be of benefit to society. For doing so society rewards him according to the socialist rule: "From each according to his ability, to each according to his work."

Socialist society deals sternly with slackers, loafers and others who would like to live by the labour of others. To them the Stalin Constitution applies the motto: "He who does not work, neither shall he eat."

The position of the working people in socialist society stimulates them, and the Constitution makes it their duty to perform with honour the work assigned to them, steadily to raise the productivity of their work and to combat with all their energy the old-fashioned views on work that still survive.

In Soviet socialist society work is the foundation of the national wealth and the personal well-being of the citizen, the basis upon which the might of the Soviet Union rests.

THE MORAL AND POLITICAL UNITY OF SOVIET SOCIETY

On January 17, 1939, a general census of the country was taken. It appeared that the population of the Soviet Union was 170,000,000 in round figures. Half of this number were workers and other employees (with their families), and somewhat less than half were either collective farmers or handicraftsmen united into co-operatives. Individual peasants and handicraftsmen who were keeping their own private establishments but without employing any hired help accounted (with their families) for 2.5 per cent of the population.

Thus our society consists *exclusively of toilers*—workers, peasants and the intelligentsia, the ranks of which are being swelled by additions from worker and peasant stock. Moreover, the vast majority of the working people are employed in *socialist economy*—in state enterprises and government institutions, or work in co-operative or collective-farm enterprises. In our society there are no exploiting classes. This means that our society is a *socialist* society.

However, there are *two classes* in our society: the working class and the peasantry. The still persisting division into workers and peasants (the overwhelming majority of the latter being collective farmers) is explained by the fact that in our country there are two forms of socialist property, two types of socialist enterprises.

The workers and peasants belong to different but *friendly classes*. The working class is the foremost, the leading class in our society. Jointly the working class and the toiling peasants fought for their emancipation, jointly they defeated their enemies, and jointly they built the new, socialist society. Their interests coincide on all fundamental issues. And their aims are identical, too: to consolidate our state, to ensure stable, enduring peace between the nations, to work in concert for the completion of the building of Socialism and the gradual transition to Communism.

Cast a glance at our country, from end to end, and you will see what an incomparable picture of *friendly co-operation between workers, peasants and intelligentsia* our socialist society presents. You will behold a people united in purpose, a people of many millions, each helping the other like brothers, a people engaged in *one great common undertaking*.

This profound community of fundamental interests, of views and aims among the Soviet people, their solid support of the Soviet government and the Communist Party, we call the *moral and political unity* of the Soviet people. What is its origin?

This unity took shape over a long stretch of time. There was no such profound unity among the whole Soviet people when remnants of the exploiting classes still existed in our midst, when small, privately-conducted farming prevailed in the Soviet countryside. It developed gradually, in proportion as the peasants, changing into collective farmers, were drawn more and more into the building of Socialism and became increasingly conscious of the community of their interests with those of the workers, with the interests of the whole people and of the state.

Consequently, the moral and political unity of the Soviet people is rooted in the circumstance that the economic basis of our society is *uniform for all,* that all people in the Soviet Union are at work in a uniform system of socialist economy.

Its moral and political unity gives socialist society an enormous advantage over capitalist society. In the latter an irreconcilable struggle is going on between workers and capitalists, between peasants and landlords—between the exploited and the exploiters. The capitalists and landlords resort to every means of violence and oppression, including armed force, against the workers and peasants. There can, of course, be no thought of moral and political unity in capitalist society.

Class contradictions and the class struggle are the causes of the inherent instability of capitalist society. The struggle of the working class and of all toilers against the exploiting classes leads inevitably to the collapse of the capitalist system in all countries.

Our moral and political unity is reflected in the unity and friendship that exists between all Soviet peoples. It is an inexhaustible source of Soviet patriotism.

Created during the period of peaceful socialist construction, our moral and political unity was considerably enhanced during the Patriotic War.

The friendly co-operation in the U.S.S.R. between workers, peasants and intellectuals, and the moral and political unity of Soviet society, are fundamental sources of the unshakeable stability and indestructible might of the Soviet Union.

The moral and political unity of the Soviet people is vividly manifested in the love which the entire nation feels for the leader of our country, Comrade Stalin.

CHAPTER II

THE SOVIET SOCIALIST STATE

THE SOVIETS

SOVIETS came into existence as early as the Revolution of 1905, when they functioned as organs of the workers' insurrection, as embryos of a new, revolutionary power. After the Revolution of February 1917 the Soviets spread rapidly all over the country. And when in October (new style—November) 1917 the working class seized power and the rule of the capitalists and landlords was destroyed, the Soviets in consequence grew to full strength, evolved into the decisive force in the country and became the organs of state power.

The Soviets constitute the most all-embracing mass state organization, which unites all the working people of the Soviet Union regardless of sex, nationality, race, occupation, party affiliation, education, religion, etc. In the Soviets you will find Russians and Azerbaijanians, Ukrainians and Khakassi, Byelorussians and Uzbeks, Estonians and Kirghizians, old Bolsheviks and non-Party collective-farm women, world-renowned scientists and workers of elementary education, metal workers and shepherds, weavers and milkmaids, railwaymen and airmen, all sitting side by side. The Deputies to the Soviets are elected by the whole of the people. The Soviets are genuine popular government, are of the flesh and bone of the people.

Every village and hamlet, every city, every district, every area, region and territory has its Soviet.

The local Soviets are altogether different from the so-called local self-government bodies that existed in tsarist Russia and still exist in bourgeois countries. Those bodies were not and are not vested with any powers of state administration. There state power was and is exercised locally by officials appointed by the government.

The local Soviets of Working People's Deputies, from the Regional Soviet to the Village Soviet, are, under the Stalin Constitution, local *organs of state power.*

The local Soviets direct the economic, cultural and political development in their respective constituencies; draw up their budgets, ensure the maintenance of public order on their territory, the observance of the laws and the protection of the rights of citizens, and assist in enhancing the defensive capacity of the country. They elect their executive committees, which are accountable to them for all their activities. They set up departments each of which is in charge of some particular branch of state administration, such as public education, public health, local industry, trade and social maintenance.

The Soviets of Working People's Deputies elect standing committees to render practical assistance in their work. These committees closely link up the Soviets with the population, with their constituents, and enlist the broad masses in the work of administering the state.

Early in 1919 Lenin wrote that the Soviets had become the *permanent and sole foundation of all state power in our country.*

The Soviets of Working People's Deputies constitute the *political foundation* of Soviet socialist society, just as our economic enterprises, our entire socialist economy, forms the economic foundation of Soviet socialist society.

THE SOVIET REPUBLIC

Let us take any Soviet country, Uzbekistan, for example, and see how Soviet government is organized there.

All Uzbek Soviets of Working People's Deputies are united into one single national state organization in which each Soviet has its particular place, its rights and duties. This integrated national political community bears the name of Uzbek Soviet Socialist Republic. Let us take another Soviet country, say, Lithuania. All Lithuanian Soviets of Working People's Deputies are united into a single national state organization, the Lithuanian Soviet Socialist Republic. And so on.

Our Soviet country, taken as a whole, is the unification of the national Soviet Socialist Republics into a single multinational Soviet state, *the Union of Soviet Socialist Republics*.

Thus, each one of the Soviets is a component part of the unified Soviet state power.

The Soviets mean *power in the hands of the working people*. This is distinctly set forth in the Constitution of the Soviet Union:

"All power in the U.S.S.R. belongs to the working people of town and country as represented by the Soviets of Working People's Deputies."

The Constitutions of all Soviet Republics contain the same affirmation.

This means that the Soviets elected by the urban and rural population exercise *all* state power in the Union of Soviet Socialist Republics, and *all* state power in each Soviet Socialist Republic.

The Soviet citizen has every right to say, and say with justified pride: "Our state, that's we ourselves!"

The radical difference between the Soviet state and all other states consists in the fact that it has as its political foundation the mass organization of precisely those classes (workers and peasants) which in the capitalist countries are oppressed and trodden under foot by their exploiters but here are free and govern the country. In the capitalist countries state power is in the hands of the bourgeoisie; in our country, in the hands of the working people.

THE PRIMARY AND FUNDAMENTAL BASIS OF THE SOVIET STATE

The *alliance of the workers and peasants* is realized in the Soviets, in the joint state activities of the Deputies, who belong to the two classes of which our society is composed. The Bolshevik Party fought from its very inception for the unification of workers and peasants in a closely-knit alliance. And it was only by establishing and strengthening the alliance between workers and peasants that the working people of our country were able to achieve all they did.

Indeed, would it have been possible for us to defeat the capitalists and landlords if the workers and peasants had not been leagued together? Certainly not.

Would we have been able without the worker-peasant alliance to build socialist society and set up so powerful a state as the Soviet Union? Of course not.

Could the Soviet Union have emerged victorious from the difficult and grievous war against Nazi Germany and its accomplices if it had not enjoyed the support of the staunch alliance of workers and peasants? Most certainly not.

The workers were in need of this alliance, because without the peasants' support they would have been unable to defeat the capitalists and build socialist society.

The peasant masses stood in need of this alliance, because

without working-class leadership they would have been unable to triumph over the landlords and kulaks and achieve a radical improvement in their lives through the agency of the collective farm.

The workers and peasants require a close alliance in order to be able jointly to develop further the socialist system of society, steadily raise their standard of life and defend their Soviet country against all its enemies abroad.

The guiding force in the alliance between the workers and peasants is the working class. Why is this so?

The workers are concentrated in great masses in the cities and industrial centres. They work together in their thousands and even tens of thousands at the big industrial plants. This has long facilitated the combination of workers into organizations whose object it is to fight the capitalists and their rule—to fight for the worker's cause, to fight for the emancipation of those who toil.

The workers are not private owners of instruments and means of production. They have a direct interest in depriving the capitalists of their factories and mills and converting the latter into the property of a socialist state, as was done by the workers of Russia in October 1917.

Thus, the very living and working conditions favour the workers' becoming the *advanced class of society*, the class most revolutionary and class-conscious, the class best organized and steeled in the struggle against all oppression and exploitation, in the struggle for Socialism.

The position of the small farmers and peasants in capitalist society is a quite different one. They are scattered all over the countryside. They run their farms as their private enterprises. In our country, too, during the first years of Soviet government, the peasants in their vast majority remained private proprietors. The very conditions of work and of life had conspired to prevent the peasants from getting together; they had rather kept them apart. Far from facilitating union, these conditions had made it more difficult for them to organize for a concerted struggle against their immediate enemies, the landlords, let alone for fighting the tsarist-landlord regime, for fighting to reconstruct their lives along new, socialist lines.

Socialism, and Socialism alone, was able fully to meet the interests of the peasants as workfolk. However, the peasants had still to be enlightened as to the meaning of Socialism, had to be shown that the socialist system was advantageous to them. They had to be given a practical demonstration of how this system could be introduced into the countryside. This was done by the Soviet workers. They helped the peasants organize collective, socialist farming.

These are the reasons why the working class became the leader, the guide of the peasant masses in the struggle to overthrow the rule of the tsar and the landlords, in the struggle against the landlords and capitalists for Soviet power, in the struggle against the kulaks for the abolition of exploitation in the countryside and for the building of a collective, socialist economy.

Socialist society has now been built in our country, but this does not mean that the working class need no longer exercise its leadership.

We must keep on consolidating and developing our Soviet socialist society, must build Communism. We have to rehabilitate our national economy with the utmost speed in the regions laid waste by the German invasion. We must build thousands of new industrial and agricultural establishments, raise labour productivity to a still higher pitch, render life still better and more beautiful, and make our country still more powerful. We must be tireless in training *politically-*

minded and efficient members of socialist society, proficient, skilled personnel for socialist economy. We must enlist them not only from the youth but also from the adult population, and train them in schools. It is only in the recent past that socialist society was built in our country and there are still many backward people among us who have not yet been able to throw off the dead weight of their antiquated views, habits and prejudices.

Clearly the solution of these difficult problems necessitates leadership on the part of the working class, the vanguard of society.

Our society has been purged of all exploiting classes. This implies that our country contains no anti-popular force capable of pitting itself against the system of society and of state in our Soviet country. (Only isolated individuals inimical to the Soviet state are left). But after -all, the capitalist encirclement of the Soviet Union, the socialist state of workers and peasants, still exists. And we know that our Soviet land was repeatedly the object of attack by capitalist powers, in consequence of which its condition became exceedingly precarious. Nor is the danger of similar attacks in the future precluded.

Under these conditions our vanguard class, the working class, must still supply Soviet society with leadership in order to strengthen still more the economic and military might of the country.

We have seen what great importance for Soviet socialist society, for the Soviet socialist state, has attached before and attaches now to the *alliance between workers and peasants under the leadership of the working class.* Comrade Stalin said with regard to this alliance:

"This is the prime and fundamental basis of the Republic of Soviets."

GUIDANCE OF SOVIET SOCIETY BY THE STATE

In the Soviets the alliance of the working class and the peasantry takes the shape of *an alliance in the sphere of the state* between the two classes of our society. This is set forth in the very first article of the Constitution of the Soviet Union:

"The Union of Soviet Socialist Republics is a socialist state of workers and peasants."

Similarly, the Constitution of every Soviet Republic commences with an article giving legal enactment to the alliance of the workers and peasants as an alliance in the sphere of the state between these classes.

In the Soviets, among the Working People's Deputies, representatives of the working class, the peasantry and the intelligentsia are to be found. Through the agency of the Soviets, the working class welds, trains and leads the whole vast mass of the toiling population. Through the Soviets, the working class exercises state guidance of the whole of Soviet society.

The difference between our socialist system and the capitalist system consists in this, that in our country governmental guidance of society (dictatorship) is exercised by the working class, while in the capitalist countries it is exercised by the bourgeoisie. In our country, state guidance of society is exercised in the interest of all those who work, while in the capitalist countries it is exercised in the interest of the bourgeoisie.

Since the October Revolution the Soviet state, in the course of its development, has passed through two main phases, two main periods.

In the first period of development of the Soviet state its

principal objective was to suppress by armed force the counter-revolutionary activities engaged in by the classes that had been overthrown, to organize the defence of the country against foreign invaders, to restore industry and agriculture and pave the way for the abolition of the remnants of the capitalist classes. Accordingly, the activities, of the various organs of the Soviet state during this period consisted principally in stamping out the resistance of the overthrown classes within the country and in organizing defence against attack from without. Particular stress was laid by the state on the strengthening of such organs of Soviet power as answered the primary needs of the hour. These included: the People's Commissariat of Army and Navy Affairs, which was in charge of the organization and military operations of the Red Army, and the All-Russian Extraordinary Commission to Combat Counter-Revolution and Sabotage, the glorious Cheka (subsequently the G.P.U.).

During this first period, the Soviet state was confronted with still another task, that of economic organization and of cultural and educational advancement. However, the activity of the Soviet state in these fields could not at that time assume extensive proportions. Those at the helm of state had to concentrate their main forces and resources on accomplishing the principal task of the day, the defeat of the foreign invaders and of the domestic foe, the counter-revolutionaries.

This period witnessed the abolition of all exploiting classes in town and country: landlords, capitalists and kulaks.

During the second period of development of the Soviet state, its principal task was the organization of socialist economy throughout the land, the destruction of the last vestiges of the exploiting classes in town and country, the extensive development of the cultural and educational activities of Soviet bodies, the establishment of a powerful army equipped with most up-to-date engines of war and capable of repelling with crushing effect any attack from abroad.

The functions of the Soviet state underwent a corresponding change.

With the destruction of the exploiting classes and the abolition of the exploitation of man by man, the necessity of military suppression within the country ceased, as there was no longer anyone to suppress. This aspect of the functions of the Soviet state became superfluous, defunct. But the country's need of military defence against attacks from without remained, and consequently such organs of the Soviet state as the Soviet Army and Navy were retained and strengthened. Also retained were the punitive organs and the intelligence department, which are necessary to ferret out and punish spies, wreckers and assassins sent into our country by capitalist powers. The *functions of the Soviet state in the field of economics, organization, education and culture* were preserved and developed to the full: new industrial enterprises were built; in particular, huge steel mills and machine-building plants were provided with the most modern equipment. Large state farms were laid out and supplied with the latest machinery. Then there was the aid extended to the peasants in the organization and consolidation of collective farms; the raising of the productivity of labour; the extension and improvement of the transport and communications systems; the increase and improvement of the country's supply of food and manufactured goods; the amplification of the network of institutions devoted to public education, public health, science, art, the press, etc.

During this period, the Soviet state acquired a new function: the *protection of public, socialist property*, which had become the basis of the whole Soviet system, the basis of the country's powerful national defence, and of the welfare of the popular masses.

The peaceful development of the Soviet Union was interrupted by the sudden perfidious attack unleashed against it by Nazi Germany and its accomplices in banditry. At this critical juncture so fraught with responsibility, the political leaders of our country, headed by Comrade Stalin, displayed titanic energy and steadfastness of purpose, great wisdom and perspicacity. They succeeded in rapidly placing all Soviet bodies and economic enterprises on a war footing. They inspired and rallied the whole people, and concentrated all its strength and resources on the paramount task of defeating the Nazi invaders, organizing the uninterrupted supply of the Soviet Army with superior military equipment and steadily replenishing the ranks with well-trained men. They placed the direction of military operations in most competent hands. All this ensured the victory of our country over its powerful foe.

During the war the supreme task of the Soviet state was to defend the country against the onslaught of its foreign enemies, the German fascist invaders. But immediately following the victory over the enemy the Soviet scene was seething with activity directed toward the rehabilitation and further development of the national economy and of culture in the U.S.S.R.

During the years of war the Soviet structure of state proved to be the best for mobilizing all the forces of the people in order to deliver crushing blows upon the enemy while repelling his attacks. And in peacetime the Soviet structure of state is best adapted for organizing the country's economic and cultural advancement.

THE SUPERIORITY OF THE SOVIET STATE OVER THE CAPITALIST STATES

The Great Patriotic War has made particularly clear to the whole world the vast superiority of the Soviet socialist state over the capitalist states. What does this superiority consist in?

The Soviet system has, first and foremost, the advantage of being close to the people, of being in direct contact with them. The Soviet system rests on the support of the popular masses. The bourgeois system has no such support. It cannot secure the firm backing of the workers, farmers and peasants whom the bourgeoisie exploits and oppresses.

Owing to the inseparable bonds that link them to the masses, the Soviets constitute the most authoritative state power in the world; they enjoy the full confidence and affection of the people. In the capitalist countries the masses have no confidence in or love for the state power; its "authority" there rests primarily on the exercise of force against the masses and the practice of deceiving them.

The Soviets have aroused the masses of the people to political consciousness. The revolutionary energy and creative initiative of the people are an inexhaustible source of strength of the Soviet state. At every difficult juncture the Soviet state makes a direct appeal to the masses, who always respond in their millions. Such a source of strength is beyond the dreams of any bourgeois state. The bourgeoisie throttles not only any and every revolutionary movement but even the slightest manifestation of independence on the part of the popular masses.

The Soviets unite the labouring masses of the various nationalities and races. They thereby help these masses to collaborate, to cement their ranks in a single alliance in the sphere of state. The co-operation and friendship among its peoples is a powerful factor enhancing the strength of the Soviet multinational state.

The bourgeois state has no such source of strength; nor can it have. Bourgeois rule is based on disunion among the working people of the various nationalities and races, on fanning the flames of enmity among them. Bourgeois multinational states are designed to enable the bourgeoisie of one nationality to oppress the popular masses of the other nationalities and races. This gives rise to a ceaseless struggle of the oppressed peoples for their liberation—a struggle which weakens the bourgeois multinational states and leads to their disintegration.

The Soviet state apparatus, in the wide sense of this word, consists not only of Soviets and the executive committees and commissions appointed by them but, in addition, of a multitude of diverse public organizations, which link up the organs of power and the organs of administration with the broadest masses of the people. This plainly strengthens and consolidates the Soviet state.

The bourgeois state apparatus is a body of officials entirely divorced from the people; it consists of bureaucrats who are alien and hostile to the masses, and who grind down the workers and farmers.

The Soviet state has an army whose officers and men are related to the masses by ties of blood. In a bourgeois state the army is kept apart from the people, and its officers belong to classes which are antagonistic and inimical to the mass of the soldiers.

All this yields Soviet rule yet another advantage: most comprehensive guidance of the people. In no country can bourgeois rule claim that much. The bourgeoisie can lead, can direct, but only by oppressing the toiling masses, by overcoming their resistance. And the longer this continues, the more does this resistance grow, the more difficult does it become for the bourgeoisie to govern the popular masses. This inevitably leads to the downfall of the bourgeois state.

The Soviet state is therefore an absolutely *new*, a *higher type of state power*, a type that has not existed hitherto in the history of man.

In the capitalist countries state authority is an instrument of oppression and exploitation of the labouring masses, a means for strengthening the rule of the capitalists and landlords. The state power of the Soviets served as an instrument which liberated the working people of our country from exploitation and every manner of oppression. The Soviet state was the principal and most powerful instrument in the building of socialist society in our country and is now serving as such in the building of Communism. The Soviet state is the most potent and reliable weapon for defending the interests of the working people, a weapon for defending the Soviet motherland against its foreign enemies.

The Soviet system of state, established thirty years ago, is one of the chief sources of the strength and might of the Soviet Union.

CHAPTER III

THE STATE STRUCTURE OF THE UNION OF SOVIET SOCIALIST REPUBLICS

☆

THE STATUS OF THE PEOPLES COMPOSING THE SOVIET UNION

IN THE RUSSIAN Empire, the landlords and capitalists held sway. The tsarist government was the embodiment of their rule. All peoples were oppressed by it, particularly the non-Russian nationalities, which it declared were incapable of cultural development and self-government.

The tsarist regime carved up and recarved the country as best suited its own interests and convenience in governing and oppressing the peoples of Russia. The national interests of the various peoples were not taken into consideration at all. It was by no means rare for the boundary line of a province to cut straight across the territory of this or that nationality.

Soviet rule put an end to national oppression and abolished the old tsarist administrative divisions of the country. Lenin and Stalin, the founders of the Soviet state, and the whole Bolshevik Party strove from the very first to give each Soviet people a full opportunity freely to arrange its own life, to create its own national state structure. At the same time Lenin and Stalin strove for voluntary union of all Soviet peoples in one powerful federal Soviet state.

In the practice of building the Soviet state four forms of national state structure have been evolved within which the various Soviet peoples live their lives: 1. *Union Republics,* 2. *Autonomous Republics,* 3. *Autonomous Regions, and* 4. *National Areas.*

Why such a diversified pattern of national statehood in our country?

About 60 nations and nationalities live in the Soviet Union. They all differ from each other in language and customs, in their history and level of culture.

Some of them, like the Russians, Ukrainians, Georgians, Armenians, Uzbeks and Letts, had formed states and possessed national cultures even in ancient times. Others, such as the Mari, Komi, Oirots, Chukchi, Evenki and Nentsi, established their national state organizations only with the advent of Soviet power and only then began to develop their respective national cultures. Some of the Soviet peoples number tens of millions of members, others a few hundred thousand, and still others only some tens of thousands or even less. Clearly, with such diversity it would have been impossible and wrong for all these peoples to follow one pattern in building their national state organizations. The *specific features of each people* had by all means to be taken into account.

Each Soviet people which has set up its own national state structure—be it a Union Republic, Autonomous Republic, Autonomous Region or a National Area—manages its own internal affairs through the Deputies which it elects. At the same time it takes part, through its representatives, in managing the affairs of the Soviet Union as a whole.

Each one of the Soviet national state structures is a component part of a single multinational state, the *Soviet Union.*

WHAT IS THE SOVIET UNION?

The U.S.S.R. is made up of a number of Soviet Republics which have united to form a single state. What induced the Soviet Republics to form such a union?

Even before Soviet rule was established a certain division of labour between the various large economic regions of our country came to be historically established. For instance, the northern and central regions could not dispense with grain imported from the South, while the northern and the central regions supplied the South and East with textile goods, and the southern and eastern regions provided coal, oil and cotton for the factories and mills located in the central and northern districts.

This historically-evolved division of labour was convincing proof that not a single Soviet Republic could rapidly restore its economy and develop it further without close economic collaboration between all the Soviet Republics, without an amalgamation of their economic forces and resources.

On the other hand, the experience of the joint struggle against the counter-revolutionaries at home and the foreign invaders argued with equal conviction that no Soviet Republic could successfully defend itself singlehanded against military attack from without. This impelled the various Soviet Republics to combine their military forces and resources for the purpose of organizing a powerful unified system of defence against the capitalist encirclement.

Lastly, Soviet power, power in the hands of the working people, is of such a nature that it does not lead to disunion or strife among the nationalities, as is the case when the bourgeoisie are in power, but to their unification and friendship, to fraternal assistance, rendered by the stronger and more advanced peoples to the small and backward peoples.

Comrade Stalin briefly explained the causes and purposes of uniting the Soviet Republics into a single federal state as follows:

"All the forces of the people had to be combined for the work of building Socialism. The country had to be made impregnable. Conditions had to be created for the all-round development of every nationality in our country."

One can readily imagine in what a precarious situation the Soviet peoples would have found themselves in their fight against Nazi Germany if they had not formed as far back as 1922 a single federal state, the U.S.S.R., with a single Union-wide authority, a unified army, a unified national economy, a solid stretch of territory and a uniform system of citizenship.

But the strength of the Soviet Union does not consist solely in the fact that it is a single federal state consisting of numerous peoples. The strength and stability of the Soviet Union is also due to the fact that it is based on the most democratic principles, on the principles of genuine popular rule.

Multinational capitalist states were usually the outgrowth of conquest, subjugation or the forcible incorporation of peoples. That, for example, was how the U.S.A. and the British Empire were formed. The United States in 1803 *purchased* Louisiana from France, in 1819 *purchased* Florida from Spain, in 1845 *wrested* Texas from Mexico and by means of *war* compelled that country to sell it the territory which today constitutes the states of Utah, Arizona, New Mexico and California; in 1867 it *purchased* Alaska, including the Aleutian Islands, from the tsarist government for 14,320,000 rubles. In addition, the United States government waged over a hundred *wars* against the numerous but practically defenceless Indian tribes who were the owners of extensive territories. This led to the almost complete physical extermination of the indigenous population of the country. Such were the ways and means by which the United States increased its original territory tenfold.

The Soviet Union had a quite different origin. It was formed in 1922 by the *voluntary union* of four Soviet Republics into a single federal state. A decision to this effect was unanimously adopted by the freely elected representatives of the Soviet peoples assembled at the First All-Union Congress of Soviets.

Since then the number of Soviet Union Republics has increased to sixteen. At the present time, the Soviet Union comprises the following Union Republics:

The Russian Soviet Federative Socialist Republic (R.S.F.S.R.)
The Ukrainian Soviet Socialist Republic
The Byelorussian Soviet Socialist Republic
The Uzbek Soviet Socialist Republic
The Kazakh Soviet Socialist Republic
The Georgian Soviet Socialist Republic
The Azerbaijan Soviet Socialist Republic
The Lithuanian Soviet Socialist Republic
The Moldavian Soviet Socialist Republic
The Latvian Soviet Socialist Republic
The Kirghiz Soviet Socialist Republic
The Tajik Soviet Socialist Republic
The Armenian Soviet Socialist Republic
The Turkmen Soviet Socialist Republic
The Estonian Soviet Socialist Republic
The Karelo-Finnish Soviet Socialist Republic.

All these republics became members of the Soviet Union *in accordance with the expressed will of the people themselves.*

The voluntary nature of the unification was one of the foundations upon which the Soviet Union was formed, strengthened and developed into the powerful force that it is today. Comrade Stalin says:

"...no union of peoples, no amalgamation of peoples into a single state, can be durable unless it is based on absolutely voluntary consent, unless the peoples involved themselves desire to unite."

The Soviet Republics, which voluntarily combined to form a union, enjoy *equal rights*. All interrelations between the Soviet peoples are based, as Lenin taught us, on the humanitarian principle of equality of rights and not on the feudal principle of privileges for the chosen few, a principle destructive of human dignity. "Not a single privilege for a single nation!... Not the slightest oppression, not the slightest injustice to any national minority!" wrote Lenin.

In the Soviet Union there are no dominant or privileged nations, nor are there any subject, oppressed nations, as was the case in the Russian Empire and as is the case today in bourgeois multinational states. The peoples of the Soviet Union all have equal rights. Each Union Republic—irrespective of the people that-form it, of the population it holds, of the size of its territory—is on a par with all the other Union Republics.

Take the Russian Union Republic (R.S.F.S.R.). It is the biggest Soviet Republic both in population (over 109,000,000) and area (about 17,000,000 square kilometres). It was the first Soviet Republic to come into existence. It is the mother republic, for its territory is the birthplace of many other Union Republics.

The Russian nation has rendered invaluable service to all its sister nations in winning and strengthening Soviet power, in uniting the constituent republics into a voluntary union in which all enjoy equal rights, in building a new, free, secure and cultured life. During the Patriotic War the Russian nation, without a moment's hesitation, assumed the burden of tremendous sacrifice in order to achieve victory over Nazi Germany. Thanks to its clarity of vision, its staunchness of character and fortitude in adversity, the Russian people has come to be generally recognized, and deservedly so, as the leading force among the Soviet peoples.

Yet do the Russian people enjoy any special rights or privileges as compared with the other Soviet peoples? Of course not. The Russian Soviet Federative Socialist Republic enjoys the same rights, no more and no less, as all the other Union Republics, whose respective populations and territories are much smaller.

The equality of the Union Republics finds expression in the fact that all of them, as Comrade Stalin said, "enjoy the advantages of the Union to an equal degree." Their unification does not in the least violate any interest of the republics; on the contrary, it provides the best safeguard of the interests of each of them. Moreover, all the Union Republics benefit equally by the unification.

The *equality of the constituent Republics* furnishes another basis of the Soviet Union's might and strength.

The U.S.S.R. is *a fraternal family of Soviet nations* united voluntarily and on the basis of equality by bonds of amity and close co-operation in a single federal state.

WHAT IS A UNION REPUBLIC?

Unprecedented prosperity was achieved within a short period of time by the various Union Republics, particularly those which in tsarist Russia had been backward, despotically-ruled and nationally-oppressed border regions.

For instance, in the Kazakh Union Republic large-scale industry has reached a high degree of development. The Karaganda coal mines rank third in importance in the Soviet Union. The Republic's non-ferrous metallurgical plants (copper, lead, zinc) are the biggest in the Soviet Union. The formerly nomadic population of Central Kazakhstan has settled down. Before the war 98 per cent of all peasant farms had been organized into collective farms.

The Kazakh people have also made tremendous cultural progress. Under the tsar only two Kazakhs out of a hundred could read and write. Since the Soviets came to power attendance at schools has increased 23.5-fold. There are 60 times as many secondary schools as before the revolution. The Kazakh Republic numbers 23 higher educational institutions, of which there was a total lack before. There is also a Kazakh Academy of Sciences, comprising 42 research institutes. The masterpieces of Kazakh national literature are well known throughout the Soviet Union.

Prodigious progress also characterizes all the other Union Republics. This is to be attributed to the extensive initiative displayed by the popular masses of the Union Republics, to their free, national state structures, the leadership provided by the Communist Party of the Soviet Union, and the fraternal assistance received from the Russian people and the all-Union organs of Soviet power.

What is the state structure of the Union Republics?

A Union Republic is organized voluntarily and bears the name of the nation that founded it.

Each Union Republic is a *national Soviet socialist state of workers and peasants, which voluntarily forms a direct constituent part of the Soviet Union on the basis of equality with all the other Union Republics.* All the organs and institutions of state, higher and local, of a Union Republic transact their official business in the native language of the republic.

On becoming a member of the U.S.S.R., a Union Republic remains a *sovereign* state. This means that each Union Republic *exercises state power independently* on its own territory with regard to all questions except those jurisdiction over which it has voluntarily transferred to the all-Union organs of state power and state administration. The questions thus transferred to the jurisdiction of all-Union organs are enumerated in Article 14 of the Constitution of the U.S.S.R.

Wherein do the sovereign rights of a Union Republic find expression?

Each Union Republic reserves *the right freely to secede from the Union.* The reservation of this *right* shows with crystal clearness that the republics constituting the Union have united on a *truly voluntary basis.*

No bourgeois multinational state grants such a right to any of its constituent states or cantons, for their union was not voluntary but compulsory. The right of the constituent Soviet Republics freely to secede from the Union is the highest expression of their sovereignty.

Each Union Republic has *its own Constitution,* which is adopted by its Supreme Soviet, the highest organ of state power of the Republic, and can be amended only by it. This Constitution reflects the specific national and economic features of the Republic in question, and also its culture and its manners and customs. The only condition is that the Constitution of each Union Republic shall fully conform to the Constitution of the U.S.S.R. This is quite comprehensible when you bear in mind that each Union Republic is a member of the Soviet Union; and it is likewise quite feasible, as all Soviet Republics have a *uniform* economic and political basis.

Each Union Republic has *its own laws,* issued by the highest state authority of the Republic. These laws are binding throughout its territory. They may deal with any question concerning the Republic except questions of all-Union importance, which are regulated by laws passed by the highest state authority of the U.S.S.R. Included herein are such questions as those concerning war and peace, the admission of new republics to the U.S.S.R., and the adoption of the consolidated state budget of the U.S.S.R.

The passage of an all-Union law on any question, as, for example, a law on the basic principles governing the use of land, on health protection or education, does not preclude the passage of a Republican law on the same subject; the Republican law specifies how to apply the general principles of the all-Union law to the conditions obtaining in the particular republic. Should, however, a Republican law diverge from an all-Union law, the all-Union law prevails, being binding upon all Union Republics.

A Union Republic on joining the U.S.S.R. retains *control of its territory*. The territory of a Union Republic may not be altered without its consent, and any change in its boundaries must be confirmed by the highest state authority of the U.S.S.R.

Each Union Republic has troops of *its own*, the *Republican, military formations*. The question of the manner in which the Republican military formations are to be organized is decided by the Union Republic itself. The all-Union authorities merely lay down the guiding principles that govern the organization of the military formations of the Union Republics. The all-Union organs of state power have jurisdiction over the organization of the defence of the U.S.S.R., and direct all the armed forces of the Soviet Union. The Republican military formations are constituent parts of the armed forces of the U.S.S.R.

Each Union Republic has *the right to enter into direct relations with foreign states* to conclude agreements and exchange diplomatic and consular representatives with them.

Each Republic decides for itself with what countries it shall establish direct relations. The all-Union authorities establish merely the general procedure governing the relations of Union Republics with foreign states and conclude treaties with them in behalf of the U.S.S.R.

The laws authorizing the Union Republics to have their own military formations and establish direct relations with foreign countries, passed by the Supreme Soviet of the U.S.S.R. on February 1, 1944, signify a great extension of the sovereign rights and activities of the Union Republics. These laws imply a strengthening of the Union Republics and of the Soviet Union as a whole.

The following facts illustrate to what extent the importance of our Union Republics increased during the period of the war. Two Union Republics, the Ukrainian and the Byelorussian, which greatly contributed to the defeat of fascist Germany, were invited to attend the International Conference at San Francisco as separate and distinct powers on a par with all the other powers, for the purpose of participating in the establishment of an international organization whose object was to be the maintenance in future of lasting peace among the nations. The Ukraine and Byelorussia likewise took part in the deliberations of the Paris Peace Conference.

Each Union Republic retains its *Republican citizenship*. At the same time every citizen of a Union Republic is a citizen of the Soviet Union, and the citizens of all other Union Republics enjoy equal rights with the citizens of the given republic upon its territory. A Soviet citizen feels that any Soviet Republic he may visit is his homeland.

Emblematic of the sovereignty of each Union Republic are its distinctive *arms and flag*.

Each Soviet nation that has formed a Union Republic feels itself *absolute master* of its native land. At the same time, each Union Republic is a member of the U.S.S.R., the powerful federal state from which each Soviet nation receives, through the all-Union organs of state power, every kind of assistance to promote its political, economic and cultural development and to protect it from foreign enemies.

The Constitution of the U.S.S.R. obliges the Soviet Union to safeguard the sovereign rights of the Union Republics, and the Soviet Union discharges this obligation faithfully. When our country was attacked by Nazi Germany and its accomplices, the entire Soviet Union rose against the overweening invader. The constituent Soviet Republics occupied by the enemy were liberated and their freedom, independence and sovereign rights restored.

WHAT IS AN AUTONOMOUS REPUBLIC?

Certain localities within the confines of a Union Republic may be inhabited mainly by nationalities other than that of the Republic's basic population. They constitute minorities within the Republic concerned and possess distinctive national traits. These peoples may, by voluntary decision, form Autonomous Republics, each of which is named after the people that founded it.

Let us take, by way of illustration, one of the Autonomous Soviet Republics located in the northeastern part of European U.S.S.R., namely, in the basin of the Pechora and Vychegda Rivers. This huge country has been from time immemorial the home of the *Komi people*, who constitute the vast majority if its population. In tsarist days the Komi were dying out. They called their country "a prison," so arduous and joyless, so full of privation, misery and humiliation was the life they were compelled to lead. They repeatedly rose against their oppressors, but each uprising was cruelly suppressed.

Under Soviet rule the Komi set up their own *Komi Autonomous Soviet Socialist Republic* with *Syktyvkar* as its capital. Sawmills, canneries, lime and brick kilns, starch and molasses factories and other industrial plants sprang up. When the Patriotic War broke out a railway was laid in record time beyond the Arctic Circle; it crosses the country from the southwest to the northeast, traversing forests and swamps. Even coal mines have been sunk, though with great difficulty. They are the first in the world within the eternal ice belt. The mining town of Vorkuta, a transpolar colliery, multiplied its coal output elevenfold during the war. Oil production at Ukhta is likewise on the upgrade. The Republic's crop area has trebled. The Komi collective farms are worked with the aid of tractors and combines. Formerly even the rudiments of education were unknown to the Komi. Today all children of school age are attending school, where tuition is given in the native tongue. Ninety-seven per cent of the population are literate today. Already before the war the Republic had hundreds of primary and secondary schools, fifteen technical schools, two higher educational institutions, a base of the Academy of Sciences of the U.S.S.R., and three national theatres. Komi national literature is making progress.

Other peoples who formed their own Autonomous Republics can also record astounding progress in the development of their new, Soviet socialist life. Their achievements are the result of their own efforts, exerted within a structure of state that is free, under the leadership of the Bolshevik Party and with the fraternal assistance of the Russian nation and the central organs of Soviet power.

What is the state structure of the Autonomous Soviet Socialist Republics?

An Autonomous Republic is a *Soviet socialist national state of workers and peasants which forms part of some Union Republic* and, through it, of the Soviet Union. The R.S.F.S.R. includes the following Autonomous Republics:

The Tatar Autonomous Soviet Socialist Republic
The Bashkir Autonomous Soviet Socialist Republic
The Daghestan Autonomous Soviet Socialist Republic
The Buryat-Mongolian Autonomous Soviet Socialist Republic
The Kabardinian Autonomous Soviet Socialist Republic
The Komi Autonomous Soviet Socialist Republic
The Mari Autonomous Soviet Socialist Republic
The Mordovian Autonomous Soviet Socialist Republic
The North-Ossetian Autonomous Soviet Socialist Republic
The Udmurt Autonomous Soviet Socialist Republic
The Chuvash Autonomous Soviet Socialist Republic
The Yakut Autonomous Soviet Socialist Republic.

The Georgian Union Republic includes the following Autonomous Republics:

The Abkhazian Autonomous Soviet Socialist Republic
The Adjar Autonomous Soviet Socialist Republic.

The Azerbaijan Soviet Socialist Republic includes the Nakhichevan Autonomous Soviet Socialist Republic.

The Uzbek Soviet Socialist Republic includes the Kara-Kalpak Autonomous Soviet Socialist Republic.

While forming part of a Union Republic, each Autonomous Republic exercises state power *autonomously* within the confines of its territory. This means that the people which has formed the Autonomous Republic enjoys the right of *self-government* within its territory with regard to all questions concerning its domestic affairs. All the organs and institutions of state, higher and local, of the Autonomous Republics, use the native language of the said people in their official business.

Each Autonomous Republic has *its own Constitution*, which pays due regard to its special features. Its Constitution must be approved by the highest organ of state power of the Union Republic of which the Autonomous Republic in question forms a part. The Constitution of the Autonomous Republic must conform to the provisions of the Constitution of the U.S.S.R. as well as of the Union Republic of which the Autonomous Republic is a component part.

Each Autonomous Republic makes *its own, Republican, laws*, which are binding within its territory. The all-Union laws and the laws of the corresponding Union Republic are likewise binding within the territory of the Autonomous Republic.

Each Autonomous Republic has *its own territory*, which cannot be changed without its own consent. Any change in its boundaries must be approved by the highest organ of state power of the corresponding Union Republic.

Each Autonomous Republic has its own *citizenship, the citizenship of the Autonomous Republic*. Every citizen of an Autonomous Republic is at the same time a citizen of the corresponding Union Republic and of the U.S.S.R.

The arms and the flag of an Autonomous Republic are the same as those of the Union Republic of which it forms a part, with the addition of the *name of the Autonomous Republic*.

This state structure of the Autonomous Republics as well as the assistance rendered them by the all-Union organs of Soviet power, coupled with the assistance afforded by the Russian people and the leadership supplied by the Communist Party of the Soviet Union (Bolsheviks), explain the vast achievements of the peoples who have formed these republics. Each of these peoples is keenly aware of the indissoluble bonds that unite it with the common motherland, the Soviet Union, and is at all times ready to defend it with all its human and material resources.

WHAT IS AN AUTONOMOUS REGION?

Various parts of some of the Union Republics are inhabited by numerically small peoples which have voluntarily formed *Autonomous Regions*. The name of each of these Autonomous Regions indicates the people that constitutes the Region. The following are the Autonomous Regions included in one or other Territory of the R.S.F.S.R.: the Adygei Autonomous Region, the Jewish Autonomous Region, the Gorno-Altai Autonomous Region, the Khakass Autonomous Region, the Cherkess Autonomous Region and the Tuva Autonomous Region.

The Azerbaijan Union Republic includes the Nagorno-Karabakh Autonomous Region.

The Georgian Union Republic includes the South-Ossetian Autonomous Region.

The Tajik Union Republic includes the Gorno-Badakhshan Autonomous Region.

Let us tell the story of one of these regions.

Siberia, along the shores of the Upper Yenisei and in the valley of its tributary, the Abakan, has been from time immemorial the home of the *Khakass people*. More than a thousand years ago the Khakassi were one of the most powerful and cultured peoples in Asia. But later they were subjugated by the Mongol conquerors and lost their culture. Agriculture disappeared almost entirely among them, weeds overgrew the irrigation canals, and many crafts, the art of writing and the very name of the Khakass people fell into oblivion.

Under the tsars the Khakassi suffered cruelly at the hands of the government officials, the Russian capitalists and the native princelings and wealthy families. The Khakass people was dying out. In 1881 the *Siberian Newspaper (Sibirskaya Gazeta)* wrote that "in twenty years not a single native will be left in the valleys of the Abakan."

The Khakass people was saved from complete extinction by the Great October Socialist Revolution. The Soviet state, the Bolshevik Party and the Russian people helped the Khakassi to set up a national state organization of their own—the *Khakass Autonomous Region*. It was formed on October 20, 1930 and constitutes part of the Krasnoyarsk Territory of the R.S.F.S.R. Its regional centre is the city of *Abakan*. In 1939 the native population of Khakassia was 52,500.

The Khakass people has its own national organ of state power—the Soviet of Working People's Deputies of the Khakass Autonomous Region—and enjoys the *right of self-government* on the territory of the Region. All government bodies and institutions of the Region use the Khakass language in their official business.

The powers of the organs of state of the Region—the Regional Soviet and its Executive Committee—are set forth in a special *Ordinance Concerning the Khakass Autonomous Region*. It was drawn up by the Regional Soviet, which took into account the national specific features of the Region, and was approved by the Supreme Soviet of the R.S.F.S.R.

The other Autonomous Regions were formed analogously.

The formation of Autonomous Regions helped to increase the creative initiative and the economic and cultural development of the peoples which founded them. The history of the Khakass Autonomous Region is striking evidence of this.

Within ten years the nomad Khakassi settled down. The production of coal, gold and barytes and the processing of farm products have become large-scale industries. A timber industry has grown up; sowing areas have increased ninefold; thousands of hectares of arid soil are now irrigated by canals. Ninety-eight per cent of the peasant farms have united to form collective farms.

Almost the whole Khakass people are now literate. Khakassia has 350 schools, a pedagogical institute and three technical schools. It publishes eleven newspapers and books in hundreds of thousands of copies. The Abakan Theatre produces plays of the old Russian and West-European, as well as of Soviet, authors, including plays written by Khakassi. Khakass national literature has progressed considerably.

Similar progress has also been made by the other Soviet peoples which have formed Autonomous Regions.

WHAT IS A NATIONAL AREA?

National Areas, like Autonomous Regions, are formed voluntarily by small Soviet peoples.

They all constitute part of some Region or Territory of the R.S.F.S.R.

Their names are as follows: the Nenets National Area, the Yamalo-Nenets National Area, the Taimyr (Dolgano-Nenets) National Area, the Agin Buryat-Mongolian National Area, the Ust-Ordyn Buryat-Mongolian National Area, the Khanty-Mansi National Area, the Koryak National Area, the Chukotsk National Area, the Komi-Permyats National Area and the Evenki National Area.

Let us take one of these Areas by way of illustration. Northern Siberia, along the lower reaches of the Ob and the Taz, in the basins of the Polui, Nadim and the Pur Rivers and on the Yamal, Yavai and Gydan Peninsulas, is the age-old habitation of the *Nentsi*. When the tsar was in power the Nenets people was cruelly oppressed by his officials, by the Russian traders who came to buy up its pelts and fish, and by the owners of big reindeer herds, who formed the class of wealthy natives. The Nenets people fought valiantly against its oppressors. For a period of thirty years (1825-1856) the poorer classes of the Nentsi waged a heroic struggle, under the leadership of Vauli Piettomin and his associates, against the local tsarist authorities and against the wealthy reindeer-raisers.

The Nenets people was threatened with catastrophe. If you consult the gazetteer of 1899 you will find the following item about the Nentsi: "A tribe that is dying out, numbers 16,000 persons." The 1913 edition of the gazetteer states: "A tribe that is dying out, numbers 2,000 persons."

The Socialist Revolution prevented the utter extinction of the Nenets people. Under Soviet rule the life of this people has changed beyond recognition. On December 10, 1930, the Nentsi formed a state entity of their own—the *Yamalo-Nenets National Area*. Its chief town is *Sale-Khard*. The indigenous population of the Area was 12,000 in 1939.

More than half of the nomad population of the Area has become sedentary. Big fish-canneries and collective fisheries supplying the canneries according to contract have been set up in the Area. The collective hunting "brigades" have become the principal purveyors of pelts. The procurement of "soft gold" (pelts) has multiplied ten times over. Through cooperatives the hunters and fishermen are provided with excellent guns, fishing tackle and other equipment, with manufactured goods and with books and other cultural supplies at popular, uniform prices. The collective-farm reindeer herds are four times as numerous as before. The Area's stock-breeding industry, which was formerly confined to reindeer, now includes cattle, horses, sheep and hogs. Even agriculture—both hothouse and open field—has made its appearance in this arctic region icebound the whole year round.

In former times the local population had no medical service at all. Today this National Area has dozens of hospitals, dispensaries, medical (feldsher) and obstetrical stations.

Physicians visit patients in the tundra. Before the revolution the native population was illiterate throughout. Today this Area has 56 schools, 7 of which are secondary. Dormitories have been arranged for the children of the nomad population. The Area has a teachers' school, a reindeer-breeding college, an institute for practising co-operation, and three scientific research stations. Six newspapers are published. At the Sale-Khard House of the Nenets concerts, film shows and plays by Soviet authors, as well as Russian and foreign classics, are performed. Nenets national literature is making considerable progress.

What is the clue to these astounding successes achieved in so short a time by the Nentsi and other people of the Soviet North, successes without parallel in any other country? It is to be found in the free and creative initiative of these peoples, fostered by the Soviet national state structure under which they live. They are themselves building their new life, and are doing so under the leadership of the Communist Party, with the fraternal aid of the various all-Union organs of Soviet power. and of the great Russian people.

Each nationality which has formed a National Area enjoys on its territory the rights of *self-government* in its internal affairs. The rights and duties of the organs of state power of the National Area—the Area Soviet of Working People's Deputies and its Executive Committee—are defined in an *Ordinance Concerning National Areas* approved by the Supreme Soviet of the R.S.F.S.R.

All state organs and institutions of the National Area employ the native language of the people forming the Area in their official business.

The peoples inhabiting our northern regions warmly treasure the interests of the common Soviet motherland, of which they feel themselves a part.

THE FRIENDSHIP OF THE SOVIET PEOPLES IS INDESTRUCTIBLE

The Soviet Union, as we see, is a state based on the voluntary union of free and equal peoples. These peoples have each formed their own, national, state organization. At the same time all Soviet peoples are gathered into the fold of one single family, the members of which live in friendship and fraternal co-operation.

Such was not the system, such were not the mutual relations between the various peoples of old Russia, nor are they those of the capitalist countries of today.

Let us take, for instance, the British Empire, which British bourgeois leaders like to refer to as a commonwealth of nations. Let us see what sort of "commonwealth" this is. More than 535,000,000 people inhabit the British Empire. Of these the British account for no more than 48,000,000. Over 400,000,000 compose the populations of dependent countries oppressed by the British bourgeoisie—the colonies and semi-colonies of the Empire. India alone comprises about 800 different nationalities and tribes. The British Empire is no commonwealth of nations, but what does exist is the cruel oppression of the various peoples by the British imperialists.

Hundreds of nationalities inhabiting Asia, Africa and the Pacific Islands suffer inhuman oppression at the hands of the British, American, French, Dutch, Belgian and other bourgeoisies. But these peoples do not calmly submit to their lot; they fight incessantly and with increasing intensity against their oppressors, reaching the point of armed insurrection and the proclamation of their independence, as for instance in the case of Indonesia. They fight for a solution of the national question, that is, for the abolition of national oppression, for the right of each nation to govern its own country.

In the Soviet Union national oppression has been done away with long ago. In our country the *national question has been settled*, for the first time in history, *in a way that is just to all concerned*, by the Soviet state, under the leadership of the Communist Party.

Equality of nations has not only been legally proclaimed in our country, but introduced in practice and made part and parcel of the life of every people in the U.S.S.R. With the fraternal assistance of the entire Soviet Union each Soviet nation has brought its economy and its national culture to a high point of development; each decides its own internal affairs, and on an even plane with all other Soviet nations participates in the administration of the entire country.

Such is the state structure of the U.S.S.R., upon the basis of which there has come into existence and grown into an indestructible force the great friendship of the Soviet peoples, which Comrade Stalin called the most valuable achievement of the Soviet state and the Communist Party. As early as 1935 he said:

"... as long as this friendship exists, the peoples of our country will be free and invincible. Nothing can daunt us, neither enemies at home nor enemies abroad, as long as this friendship lives and flourishes."

The profound truth contained in these words was confirmed by the Great Patriotic War. Our enemies calculated that with the first onrush of their troops the Soviet Union would "fall to pieces." These calculations naturally proved utterly wrong. The fraternal alliance of the Soviet peoples became even stronger and more steeled during the stern years of desperate struggle against the Nazi invaders conducted under the leadership of the Bolshevik Party. Each Soviet nation dedicated all its energies, all its resources, to the sacred cause of defending the Soviet Union, to the cause of routing the enemy and ejecting him from Soviet territory, of annihilating fascism. The solidarity, the mutual confidence and the fighting alliance between the Soviet peoples is today stronger than ever.

The German fascists propagated the "theory" that mankind is divided into two unequal parts: on the one side the Germans, who they alleged belong to a "superior race," to a "nation of masters"; and on the other side all the remaining nations, who they said belong to "inferior races," to "nations of slaves."

The Soviet nations have refuted this fascist balderdash in practice. They have given practical proof of the fact that any nation, once freed from national oppression and capitalist bondage, is capable of establishing a progressive state of its own and of developing its economy and national culture to a very high pitch.

The Soviet Union, which was defending the ideas of freedom, equality and amity of nations, emerged victorious from this gruelling military conflict. But the German fascist state, which was seeking to establish the domination of one nation and to subjugate all others, suffered defeat and was destroyed.

The free union of equal Soviet peoples, created under the leadership of the Communist Party, is the mightiest and most stable state in the world.

CHAPTER IV

THE HIGHER ORGANS OF STATE POWER AND OF STATE ADMINISTRATION OF THE U.S.S.R.

☆

HOW THE ORGANS OF STATE POWER ARE FORMED IN OUR COUNTRY

THE ORGANS of state power in our country—the Soviets of Working People's Deputies—are freely elected by the whole of the people.

Formerly this was not so. In the Russian Empire supreme power was transmitted by inheritance from one tsar to the other. After the Revolution of 1905, the tsarist government, as a concession to the people, established the State Duma, which Lenin called a crass parody of popular representation. The elections to this Duma were held as follows: First electors were chosen. The landlords and urban bourgeoisie chose three-fourths of the total number of electors, the peasants chose 22.4 per cent and the workers 2.4 per cent. The electors then met to elect the deputies to the Duma. Naturally, under such a system of elections very few representatives of the workers and peasants could obtain seats in the tsarist Duma.

The women, half the population, had no right to vote altogether. The non-Russian nationalities of Central Asia and Siberia, which made up almost ten million of the population, were also wholly deprived of the right to vote. The peoples of the Caucasus were entitled to only 10 deputies. No one was eligible unless he knew Russian.

Similar limitations on the elective franchise exist even today in the bourgeois countries. Their constitutions and election laws are usually so framed that large sections of the citizenry are either entirely excluded from the electoral franchise or have their electoral rights severely restricted. Many countries have no women's suffrage. In colonies the native population is shorn of electoral rights by the dominant state.

In the capitalist countries, before anyone is granted the right to vote he usually must prove his qualification to do so. For instance, an applicant for election registration may have to show that he owns a certain amount of land or other property or has paid taxes of a certain minimum amount or the special election tax (poll tax). He may further be required to show that he has a home of his own or to prove continuous residence within the election district for a stated length of time (six months, a year, two years or even longer). He may be called upon to prove that he has an education of at least so many grades or that he knows the language of the dominant nation. Many of the states in the U.S.A. demand that a prospective voter have a knowledge of the English language. In the southern states a Negro must prove that he can read and write before he is granted the right to vote. As a result of such measures millions of Negroes in the U.S.A. are to all intents and purposes disqualified from voting.

While the electoral rights of members of the labouring classes are restricted, those who belong to the exploiting classes enjoy special privileges. For instance, in England owners of industrial and commercial establishments are entitled to vote in two election districts, the one determined by their residence, the other by the location of their business. University graduates also have two votes: where they live and where their university is located.

Direct disfranchisement and electoral restrictions operate to ensure the capitalists, the landlords and their servitors a predominance in the organs of state power. In bourgeois states the ruling classes do all in their power to prevent the toiling masses from participating in the governing of the country.

Moreover, the conditions necessary to permit working-class citizens a really free exercise of their electoral rights do not exist even where the constitution grants them such rights. The capitalists and landlords are in control of the entire state apparatus; they have at their disposal the printing presses, newspapers, radio stations, schools, universities, meeting halls and huge sums of money. And these are the very things that the labouring masses in the capitalist countries do not possess. It is, therefore, very difficult for them to organize, nominate and elect candidates for public office who will really represent the interests of labour.

In capitalist countries election campaigns are waged amidst a fierce class struggle in which the exploiting classes exert tremendous pressure on the voters. The leaders of the various bourgeois parties outdo each other in their frantic efforts to win a majority of the electorate, resorting to false promises of every description, to direct bribery, intimidation and physical violence. It is not at all rare for the candidates of bourgeois parties to win elections by downright falsification and other fraudulent methods. For instance, in the Kansas City, Missouri, election district, in which Harry Truman, the present President, received a majority, voters were rushed in trucks from polling place to polling place to swell their party's vote.

How different is the picture in our country! All Soviet citizens of voting age are granted and actually ensured the absolutely unrestricted right to vote.

Everyone knows what a festive occasion for the whole people the elections to the Soviets are. Each election is preceded by a lengthy campaign, punctuated by well-attended meetings of the voters throughout the length and breadth of the country. These meetings serve to nominate the candidates for the various Soviets.

In the first elections to the Supreme Soviet of the U.S.S.R., held in 1937, 94,000,000 voters were registered in the voters' rolls. Of these, 96.8 per cent went to the polls. Communists and non-Party people nominated candidates jointly and about 98 per cent of all the votes cast were in favour of these candidates.

In these elections to the Supreme Soviet of the U.S.S.R. and in the subsequent elections to the Supreme Soviets of the Union and Autonomous Republics and to the local Soviets, more than 1,400,000 Deputies were chosen. This means that the people nominated and elected almost a million and a half of their finest representatives to govern the country.

The second elections to the Supreme Soviet of the U.S.S.R. took place on February 10, 1946. The number of voters had now reached a total of 101,000,000. 99.7 per cent of the electorate took part in these elections, and over 99 per cent of the ballots cast favoured the candidates nominated jointly by Communists and non-Party people.

In the second elections to the Supreme Soviets of the Union and Autonomous Republics, which took place in February 1947, 104,000,000 citizens were entitled to vote. Of these over 99 per cent went to the polls and over 99 per cent of the votes cast were in favour of the candidates nominated by the bloc of Communists and non-Party people.

Not a single bourgeois country can boast such almost one hundred per cent participation in public elections or such unanimity of the electorate. In Great Britain, for instance, only 75 per cent of the electors voted in the last elections to parliament. And in the United States only 37.5 per cent of the voters went to the polls in the last elections to Congress.

In no capitalist country has there ever been a case of the ruling bourgeois party forming an election bloc with the masses unaffiliated to any party. The bourgeois parties do not trust the popular masses, but on the contrary are afraid of them.

Only a Communist Party can venture to form an election alliance with non-Party masses, for it trusts them and they trust it. Only in the Land of Socialism, the land of genuine democracy, can an alliance of Communists and non-Party people prove such a splendid election success.

The elections to the Soviets are proof of the profound moral and political unity of the Soviet people, of their unanimity and their solidarity with the Soviet government and the Communist Party.

The election to the Soviets are a magnificent demonstration of the unbounded confidence and love of the people of the Soviet Union for the Communist Party and its leader, Comrade Stalin.

What are the principles which in our country govern the elections to the organs of state power, the Soviets?

The Stalin Constitution introduced *universal suffrage*. It contains no discrimination against women. Under its provisions women have the same electoral rights as men. The very idea of depriving them or restricting them in these rights seems preposterous and outrageous to the Soviet citizen.

The Soviet Constitution does not curtail any citizen's electoral or other rights because of the language that he speaks or the colour of his skin. Whether he is a Russian, a Bashkir, a Ukrainian, an Estonian, a Byelorussian, an Uzbek, an Avar, a Nenets, a Komi, a Mari or an Uigur, he has the right to vote and be voted for in all elections to public office under Soviet rule.

The Soviet Constitution does not differentiate between citizens according to their social origin. A citizen may belong to the category of worker or peasant—collective or individual farmer—or he may be a member of the intelligentsia or come from one of the exploiting classes that formerly existed in our country. All citizens possess the electoral franchise irrespective of their social origin, property status and former occupation.

Whether a citizen has a higher, a secondary or an elementary education or no education at all is immaterial in determining his right to vote, and he likewise is entitled to vote regardless of the religion he practises or his failure to practise any.

Whether a citizen has a permanent place of residence or frequently changes his address does not in the least affect his right to participate in the elections at the polling place of the election district in which he happens to be on the day of the elections.

Service in the Soviet Army or Navy does not deprive a citizen of his right to cast his ballot at the place where his army unit or ship is stationed.

Thus in our country all citizens of voting age are entitled to vote, without any restriction whatever.

The sole and quite natural exceptions are insane persons and persons who have been convicted by a court of law and whose sentences include deprivation of electoral rights for a fixed period.

The right to elect members of the various Soviets is

enjoyed by every citizen of the Soviet Union who has reached the age of 18.

Any Soviet citizen who is 23 years of age may be elected a member of the Supreme Soviet of the U.S.S.R. Any citizen of the Soviet Union may, on attaining the age of 21, be elected a member of the Supreme Soviet of any Union or Autonomous Republic, according to its constitution, and a member of any local Soviet on attaining the age of 18.

The Stalin Constitution provides for *equal suffrage*. This means that no citizen enjoys any special rights or privileges in elections to the Soviets. Peasants have the same rights as workers, women the same as men; professional people, scientists and men in the armed forces have the same rights as all other citizens. The right of suffrage is the same for everybody: each voter has one vote.

This equality in the matter of suffrage strengthens the moral and political unity of Soviet society, enhances the friendly co-operation among workers, peasants and intellectuals and hence also the might of the Soviet state.

Under the Stalin Constitution elections to all organs of state power are *direct*. This means that the voters do not vote for "electors" who do the final choosing, but vote directly for the candidates they prefer. The principle of the direct vote applies not only to elections for the village, city, district, regional and other local Soviets but also to the Supreme Soviets of the Union and Autonomous Republics and to the Supreme Soviet of the Union of Soviet Socialist Republics.

Direct elections make it possible for the Soviet voter to be well-informed about the candidates for whom he casts his vote in not only the elections to the local organs of state power but also the elections to the supreme organs of the Soviet Republics and to the supreme organ of the entire Soviet Union. Direct elections strengthen the ties between the voters and all the organs of state power, and also help to improve the work of elective bodies.

The Stalin Constitution established the principle of the *secret ballot* in the elections to all the Soviets. This means that no one has a right to know for whom a voter casts his vote. No one, not even a member of the election commission, may be present inside the special booths provided for voters to mark their ballots. Each voter freely decides for himself whether any particular candidate deserves his confidence or not. This procedure ensures complete freedom of elections.

Who may nominate candidates for the Soviets?

This right is possessed by all public organizations and societies of the working people: Communist Party organizations, trade unions, co-operatives, youth organizations and cultural societies, as well as general meetings of workers and other employees voting by establishments, of servicemen voting by army units, of peasants voting by collective farms, villages and volosts, and of workers and other employees of state farms voting by state farms.

Hence, it is the popular masses themselves who nominate the candidates for the office of Soviet Deputy. They also present their *mandates* to their future Soviet Deputies.

Our Constitution establishes constant contact between a Deputy and his constituency. It gives the constituents the right to demand of their Deputy that he *account* to them for the way he is fulfilling their election mandate, that he report on the work of the Soviet to which he is elected.

Soviet voters do not confine themselves to electing Deputies every so many years to organs of state power and then return to their routine tasks. Soviet electors follow up the work of their Deputies, check up on it, and if any Deputy should deviate from the right path and forfeit the confidence reposed in him they may make use of their *right to recall the Deputy* before the expiration of his term of office, and elect another in his place, as our constitution specifies.

The constitutions of bourgeois countries contain no such provision. There, once the elections are over and the successful candidates have taken their seats, all relations between them and their constituencies are usually at an end. No sooner are candidates of bourgeois parties installed in office than they forget their election promises and carry out in Parliament, Congress or legislature the will of the bourgeoisie.

A Soviet Deputy, as Comrade Stalin pointed out, is a *servant of the people;* it is his duty to carry out the will of his constituents.

Comrade Stalin advised the voters to demand of their Deputies that they remain equal to their tasks, that in their work they should not sink to the level of political philistines, that they should constantly keep before them the immortal image of the great Lenin.

The chosen of the Soviet people should, as public figures, be as clear and definite as Lenin was.

They should be as fearless in battle and as merciless to the enemy as Lenin was.

In case of danger they should be as free from any semblance of panic as Lenin was.

In deciding complex problems they should be as wise and deliberate as Lenin was.

They should be as upright and honest as Lenin was.

They should love their people as Lenin did.

Indeed, all Deputies must learn to become public figures like Lenin was, like Comrade Stalin, our beloved leader and friend of the working people, is.

THOSE WHOM THE PEOPLE HAVE ENTRUSTED WITH SUPREME POWER IN THE COUNTRY

In the elections to the Supreme Soviet of the U.S.S.R., held on February 10, 1946, 1,339 Deputies were elected. Let us see whom the people have entrusted with supreme power in the country. The Stalin election district of the city of Moscow elected as its Deputy to the Supreme Soviet of the U.S.S.R. the beloved leader of the Soviet peoples and of the Communist Party, *Joseph Vissarionovich Stalin*.

Other prominent leaders of the Soviet Union and the Communist Party, well-known throughout the country, were likewise elected Deputies to the Supreme Soviet of the U.S.S.R., such as: *V. M. Molotov, M. I. Kalinin, N. M. Shvernik, A. A. Zhdanov, A. A. Andreyev, A. I. Mikoyan, L. M. Kaganovich, K.E.Voroshilov, N.S.Khrushchev, L.P.Beriya, G.M.Malenkov, N. A. Voznesensky, N. A. Bulganin,* and *A. N. Kosygin*.

The Supreme Soviet of the U.S.S.R. includes people of distinction who stem from workers, peasants and the intelligentsia, leaders in industry and collective farming, representatives of science and culture, men from the ranks and the highest army commanders.

The list of Deputies to the Supreme Soviet of the U.S.S.R. includes, for instance, *Ivan Stepanovich Konev,* Marshal of the Soviet Union, a native of the village of Lodaino, Vologda Gubernia, who had served in the artillery during the First World War.

During the Civil War he joined the Red Army and has served in it ever since. Upon the termination of that war he attended the Higher Military Academic Courses and later the Frunze Military Academy, graduating from both.

Konev employed his military gifts with conspicuous success throughout the Patriotic War with fascist Germany. When the

Germans were being routed near Moscow he, commanding the troops of the Kalinin Front, put to flight the left flank of the enemy which was driving toward the capital. A year later he was in command of the Steppe Front, where, acting in unison with other fronts, he smashed the Belgorod-Kharkov group of the Germans. He led the remarkable encircling operation that ended in the defeat of the German troops in the Korsun-Shevchenko sector.

In May 1944 Konev, put in command of the troops of the First Ukrainian Front, led them westward into Germany. His men were the first to force the Vistula; they traversed the whole of Poland and took part in the storming of Berlin. Then, on orders from the Supreme High Command, he executed a manoeuvre far within Czechoslovakia and freed Prague, the capital of that country.

Take *Sidor Artemovich Kovpak*, Deputy to the Supreme Soviet of the U.S.S.R. He is of Zaporozhye Cossack stock and was a private in the old army. In the Civil War he fought under Chapayev. When the Patriotic War broke out, he held the post of City Soviet President in his native town of Putivl, in the Ukraine. On the approach of the Germans he went underground and organized a guerilla detachment. Soon the fame of his exploits resounded throughout the Ukrainian steppes and the Bryansk forests. The Germans were in mortal fear of him and popular legends arose about him. His guerilla detachments were gaining strength. In August 1942 he was entrusted with an important military mission by Comrade Stalin: to conduct a formidable raid with his partisans in the enemy's rear through all of the Ukraine and Byelorussia up to the Carpathian Mountains.

The partisans received from the "mainland" (Soviet territory) all they needed for their expedition, including trench mortars, anti-tank rifles and guns. Kovpak's unexampled raid, covering 10,000 kilometres of ground far in the Nazi rear, spread panic in the ranks of the enemy, and played havoc with the Nazi supply lines which brought men and equipment from Germany to the enemy troops at the Volga and in the Caucasus. On the other hand, it rejoiced the hearts of the Soviet citizens who had fallen into German bondage, and spurred them on to fight the fascist invader. This celebrated partisan leader, twice awarded the title of Hero of the Soviet Union and now a major general, was elected a Deputy to the Supreme Soviet by the Ukrainian collective farmers of the Glukhov election district.

Then there is *Sergei Ivanovich Vavilov,* also a Deputy to the Supreme Soviet of the U.S.S.R. He is one of the most prominent figures in the realm of Soviet science. An eminent physicist and Stalin Prize recipient he is President of the U.S.S.R. Academy of Sciences. During the war he energetically assisted in the work of the People's Commissariat of Armaments. He supervised the making of intricate optical instruments which excellently served the defenders of our country on land and sea. Vavilov is also widely known as the author of numerous popular scientific publications. As Deputy to the Supreme Soviet of the R.S.F.S.R., he won the love and esteem of his Leningrad constituents.

The Kirov election district of Leningrad sent as its representative in the Supreme Soviet of the U.S.S.R. a former factory hand by the name of *Kuzma Emelyanovich Titov,* of old proletarian stock. He virtually grew up in the Putilov (now Kirov) Plant, where he heard Lenin deliver some of his fiery speeches. They left an indelible mark on the soul of this young worker, and it was here that he joined the Bolshevik Party. After the October Revolution Titov attended a boiler and turbine makers' evening trade school and became superintendent of the machine shop. From the very beginning of the war he displayed the greatest self-sacrifice in the fulfilment of the tasks set by the government concerning the defence of Leningrad. Despite constant bombardment the factory continued to produce tanks for the city's valiant defenders. The tankmen would drive straight from the factory gates to the front-line positions. When part of the Kirov Plant was evacuated to the Urals, Titov accompanied it and at the new factory site became one of the organizers of the production of new types of fighting machines, the famous "KV" and "JS" heavy tanks.

Pasha N. Angelina, the chief of a women's tractor brigade at the Staro-Beshevo Machine and Tractor Station in Stalino Region, was one of the women elected to the Supreme Soviet of the U.S.S.R. She has been operating tractors for upward of fifteen years, and during this period has taught about a hundred young men and women the proper way to operate a tractor. No wonder the collective farmers thereabouts say that wherever Pasha is there is bound to be a bumper crop. She holds the wheeled-tractor efficiency record and her team came out on top in an all-Union contest among women tractor brigades.

The collective farmers of the Bairam-Ali election district in the Turkmen Republic elected *Aga-Yusup Ali*, a former *chairiker* (farm hand) to represent them in the Supreme Soviet of the U.S.S.R. Once the leader of the poor peasants of the Er-Sary-Yab *aul*, he is now a noted cotton grower, an efficient organizer, and has been elected many times in succession chairman of the Bolshevik, one of Turkmenistan's best collective farms.

Georgi Fedorovich Timushev is one of the youngest members of the Supreme Soviet of the U.S.S.R. He is only twenty-three, the son of a village feldsher, a Komi by nationality, hailing from the village of Ustnem, Ust-Kuloma District, Komi Autonomous Soviet Socialist Republic. He was attending the Pedagogic Institute at Syktyvkar when the war broke out whereupon he transferred to a military engineering school. In January 1942, we find him in command of a sapper platoon with which he advanced from Stalingrad to Hungary, where he was severely wounded. He was promoted to a lieutenancy and the title of Hero of the Soviet Union was conferred upon him. When the war ended he returned to his studies. The Komi Autonomous S.S.R. electorate made him their Deputy to the Supreme Soviet of the U.S.S.R.

These few examples will suffice to illustrate the kind of people the Soviet voters have entrusted with the governance of the country.

The Supreme Soviet of the U.S.S.R. is composed as follows: 38 per cent are wageworkers, 26 per cent are peasants and 36 per cent are office workers and intellectuals. Two hundred and seventy-seven are women, 293 are between the ages of 23 and 35. Men in the armed forces also account for a considerable group. More than four-fifths of the Deputies are Communists, the rest are non-Party people.

Parliaments in bourgeois countries are cut to a quite different pattern. Of the 437 Deputies in the Fourth State Duma of tsarist Russia, only 65 were "agriculturists" (predominantly kulaks), while eleven were workers or handicraftsmen. All the remaining Deputies were either landlords, capitalists, officials, bourgeois intellectuals or members of the clergy. As a matter of fact, there were only five genuine representatives of the working people in the Duma, and they were Bolshevik workers; yet even this handful the tsarist government exiled to Siberia.

At the present time parliaments in bourgeois countries are of a similar class composition. In the United States, for instance, Congress consists almost entirely of capitalists, a considerable number of bourgeois intellectuals, who serve the interests of the big capitalist corporations, and a few big landowners.

Our country is governed by its finest sons and daughters, by Party and non-Party Bolsheviks who have earned the confidence of the masses by their services to the state and to society, by their unstinted labour in factory, mill, mine and field, by their accomplishments in science, technology or culture, by their heroism in combatting the enemies of the Soviet motherland.

THE SUPREME SOVIET OF THE U.S.S.R.

Article 14 of the Constitution of the U.S.S.R. sets forth the precise rights possessed by the higher organs of state power and of state administration of the Soviet Union. These rights are exercised by the Supreme Soviet of the U.S.S.R. in so far as they are not assigned by the Constitution to the jurisdiction of other organs of the Soviet Union that are accountable to the Supreme Soviet of the U.S.S.R.

The Supreme Soviet of the U.S.S.R. has the exclusive right to *pass all-Union laws.* No other organ of state has this right. The following are examples of all-Union legislation: the law prescribing universal military service, adopted in 1939; the laws passed in August 1940 to admit three new Union Republics to the fraternal family of Soviet peoples, namely, the Republics of Lithuania, Latvia and Estonia; the laws extending the rights of the Union Republics in the sphere of defence and foreign relations.

An all-Union law is an expression of the will of all the Soviet nations, and takes the form of a decision of the Supreme Soviet of the U.S.S.R. All-Union laws are of binding force in all Union Republics. All public authorities, all institutions, organizations, officials and private citizens must give effect to them. They are published in the languages of all Union Republics.

The Supreme Soviet of the U.S.S.R. alone has the right to amend the Constitution of the U.S.S.R., exercise control over its observance and ensure conformity of the Constitutions of the Union Republics with the Constitution of the U.S.S.R.

The Supreme Soviet of the U.S.S.R. alone has the right to admit new republics to the Soviet Union, confirm alterations of boundaries between Union Republics and the formation of new autonomous republics, and new territories and regions.

The Supreme Soviet of the U.S.S.R. is authorized to appoint investigating and auditing commissions on any question, the requirements of which must be complied with by all institutions and officials.

The Supreme Soviet of the U.S.S.R. adopts a consolidated state budget for the whole country and the report on its execution. It contracts and grants loans, decides the more important questions regarding relations with foreign countries, and questions of war and peace, ratifies treaties with foreign states, organizes the country's defence and directs the armed forces of the Soviet Union.

Thus, the Supreme Soviet of the U.S.S.R. is *the highest organ of state power in the Union of Soviet Socialist Republics*. No organ of state power in our country is superior to the Supreme Soviet of the U.S.S.R. or is vested with equal authority.

The Supreme Soviet of the U.S.S.R. consists of *two Chambers*. One of them is called the *Soviet of the Union*, the other, the *Soviet of Nationalities*.

Both Chambers are elected on the basis of universal, equal and direct suffrage by secret ballot. The Deputies to the *Soviet of the Union* are elected by the entire citizenry throughout the U.S.S.R. on the basis of one Deputy for every 300,000 of the population. Deputies to the *Soviet of Nationalities* are voted for separately by Union Republics (on the basis of 25 Deputies from each), by Autonomous Republics (eleven Deputies from each), by Autonomous Regions (five deputies from each) and by National Areas (one Deputy from each).

The two Chambers of the Supreme Soviet of the U.S.S.R. *have equal rights*. Each of them has the right to initiate legislation, that is, to suggest new legislation and introduce corresponding bills. A law is considered adopted if passed by both Chambers by a simple majority vote in each. Amendments to the Constitution, however, require a majority of not less than two-thirds of the votes cast in each of the Chambers. The term of office of the members of both Chambers is four years. The Chambers are convened and hold their sessions simultaneously.

It may be asked: Why does the Supreme Soviet of the U.S.S.R. consist of two Chambers and not of one?

Because our state is *multinational*.

The main interests of the citizens of the Soviet Union, without distinction of nationality or race, are identical, *common*. All Soviet people are vitally interested in the strengthening of the economic and defensive might of the Soviet Union, in the establishment of prolonged and enduring peace between all countries, in seeing that the life of all Soviet peoples becomes richer and more beautiful each day.

These common interests of all Soviet citizens are represented in the supreme organ of our state by the Deputies to the *Soviet of the Union*.

But the citizens of the various nationalities and races inhabiting the Soviet Union have, besides, their own *special* interests arising out of the specific national features of each people, the peculiarities of its language, life and culture.

These special interests of the various nations are represented in the supreme organ of our state by the Deputies to the *Soviet of Nationalities*.

It is the purpose of the Soviet of Nationalities that each

of the numerous Soviet peoples which have organized national state structures of their own be enabled through its special representatives to express directly in the Supreme Soviet of the U.S.S.R. its special, national interests.

A proposal providing for such a structure of the supreme organ of state power of the U.S.S.R. was introduced by Comrade Stalin in 1923. Referring to the necessity of creating a Soviet of Nationalities as part of the supreme organ of power, Comrade Stalin said:

"Under the conditions prevailing in our Union, which embraces not less than 140,000,000 people, of whom about 65,000,000 are non-Russians—one cannot, comrades, in such a state, govern without having before us here, in Moscow, in the supreme organ, emissaries of these nationalities...."

Such a structure of the Supreme Soviet of the U.S.S.R. assures the fullest and most accurate expression of the interests of all the peoples of our country in the highest organ of state power. Such a structure of the Supreme Soviet of the U.S.S.R. facilitates the consolidation of fraternal co-operation and strengthens the bonds of friendship between all the Soviet peoples.

Bourgeois countries also have two Chambers in their Parliaments or Assemblies. They are referred to as Upper and Lower Chamber or House: the House of Lords and the House of Commons, Senate and House of Representatives, etc. In tsarist Russia, there was a State Council and a State Duma.

But the Chambers of the Supreme Soviet of the U.S.S.R. have nothing in common with the two-chamber system in bourgeois countries.

In the first place, there both chambers are organs of bourgeois power, while our chambers are organs of a Soviet socialist state. Moreover, in bourgeois countries the upper chambers are so constituted as to make it particularly difficult for the labouring masses to be represented there. These upper chambers enjoy special rights and privileges withheld from the lower chambers. In old Russia, half of the Upper Chamber (the State Council) was appointed by the tsar from among men of the most exalted station; the other half was elected by societies of the nobility, landowners, industrialists and merchants. About the same thing still holds true today of many bourgeois countries. For instance, in Great Britain the House of Lords—this remnant of the Middle Ages—consists of members of the nobility—princes of the royal blood, dukes, counts, barons—and also of archbishops and bishops. The members of the House of Lords hold their seats by right of inheritance, save the few who are appointed by the king. All laws passed by the lower chambers must also pass the upper chambers, which are given the right to delay legislation. The upper chambers hamper all progress.

Nothing of the kind exists or can exist in our Soviet Union. Both Chambers of the Supreme Soviet of the U.S.S.R. enjoy equal rights. The Soviet of Nationalities promotes the economic, political and cultural advancement of the National Republics, Regions and Areas. It represents the special interests of the free Soviet peoples in the supreme organ of the Union of Soviet Socialist Republics.

The Soviet of the Union and the Soviet of Nationalities together constitute the *single all-Union supreme organ of state power* in our country—the Supreme Soviet of the Union of Soviet Socialist Republics, which fully and accurately expresses the will of all Soviet peoples.

* * *

The citizens of each Union Republic elect their own *Supreme Soviet*, which is the highest organ of state power of the Republic. The Supreme Soviet of a Union Republic passes the laws of the Republic and is vested with such other powers as are set forth in detail in the Constitution of the Republic in question.

The Supreme Soviet of a Union Republic consists of but *one* Chamber. In the Union Republics there is no need for two Chambers. The Autonomous Republics, Autonomous Regions and National Areas composing part of a Union Republic can express their special, national interests directly in the supreme organ of the U.S.S.R. through their Deputies in the Soviet of Nationalities.

In each Autonomous Republic, its citizens likewise elect their own *Supreme Soviet*, which is the highest organ of state power in the Republic. The Supreme Soviet of an Autonomous Republic has one Chamber. Its powers are defined in detail in the Constitution of the Autonomous Republic in question.

THE PRESIDIUM OF THE SUPREME SOVIET OF THE U.S.S.R.

The Supreme Soviet of the U.S.S.R. functions during the two sessions for which it is convened annually. Special sessions may also be held. Upon completion of the business of the session, the Deputies disperse and resume their ordinary duties.

It is therefore clear that the current business of governing the state requires additional higher organs of state. What are these organs?

With one of them we are all well acquainted through its decrees, namely, the *Presidium of the Supreme Soviet of the U.S.S.R.*

The Presidium of the Supreme Soviet of the U.S.S.R. is elected at a joint session of both Chambers from among the Deputies, and consists of a President, sixteen Vice-Presidents (corresponding to the number of Union Republics), a Secretary and fifteen members. The Presidium of the Supreme Soviet of the U.S.S.R. is *accountable* to the Supreme Soviet for all its activities.

The first session of the Supreme Soviet of the U.S.S.R. held in 1937 elected as the President of the Presidium M. I. Kalinin, who headed the highest body of the Soviet state uninterruptedly from 1919 to 1946.

He died on June 3 of that year. He enjoyed tremendous popularity and was greatly loved by the people of the Soviet Union. *N. M. Shvernik*, the Deputy from the Sverdlovsk election district, was then unanimously elected to the Presidency of the Presidium.

The powers of the Presidium of the Supreme Soviet of the U.S.S.R. are set forth in the Constitution. The Presidium convenes the sessions of the Supreme Soviet of the U.S.S.R., appoints new elections to the Supreme Soviet of the U.S.S.R. and convenes the first session of the newly elected Supreme Soviet of the U.S.S.R.

In special cases, namely, if any disagreement should arise on any issue between the Soviet of the Union and the Soviet of Nationalities and the two Chambers should be unable to settle the matter, the Presidium, on the authority of Article 47 of the Constitution of the U.S.S.R., dissolves the Supreme Soviet before the expiration of its term and orders new elections.

The Presidium of the Supreme Soviet of the U.S.S.R. issues *decrees*, which, like the laws passed by the Supreme Soviet of the U.S.S.R., have equal force in all Soviet Republics. But the decrees of the Presidium of the Supreme Soviet of the U.S.S.R. must be based on the all-Union laws in operation and must come within their purview. This distinguishes a decree from a law.

The Presidium of the Supreme Soviet of the U.S.S.R. *interprets* all-Union laws—explains their purposes, the duties they impose and the methods of properly applying their provisions.

The Presidium of the Supreme Soviet of the U.S.S.R. conducts referendums, that is, on its own initiative or upon the demand of one of the Union Republics submits proposed legislation to popular discussion and vote. In this way the people themselves are given the right, in certain cases, to adopt (or reject) bills on particularly important questions.

The Presidium of the Supreme Soviet of the U.S.S.R. appoints and removes the *High Command of the armed forces of the Soviet Union,* orders partial or general *mobilization,* proclaims *martial law* in separate localities or throughout the U.S.S.R. in the interest of the defence of our country or for the purpose of ensuring public order and the security of the state.

In the intervals between sessions of the Supreme Soviet of the U.S.S.R., the Presidium proclaims *a state of war* in the event of military attack on the U.S.S.R. or when necessary to fulfil international treaty obligations concerning mutual defence against aggression.

We all know how the Presidium of the Supreme Soviet of the U.S.S.R. exercised its powers in defence of our country. On the very day that fascist Germany launched its *sudden* predatory attack against the Soviet Union, the Presidium issued four decrees: a) mobilizing citizens subject to military service in a number of areas; b) concerning martial law; c) declaring martial law in a number of republics, regions and separate cities; d) concerning military tribunals in localities placed under martial law and in regions where hostilities were going on.

In the intervals between sessions of the Supreme Soviet

of the U.S.S.R., the Presidium is authorized to release and appoint ministers, form new ministries and new regions and territories. Such decrees are submitted for confirmation to the next session of the Supreme Soviet of the U.S.S.R.

The Presidium issues decrees on questions such as those enumerated above in the intervals between sessions of the Supreme Soviet when rendered necessary by the *urgency* of the occasion.

The Presidium of the Supreme Soviet annuls decisions and orders of the Council of Ministers of the U.S.S.R. and of the Councils of Ministers of the Union Republics if they do not conform to law.

The Presidium of the Supreme Soviet of the U.S.S.R. represents the Soviet Union in its relations with foreign states; it ratifies and denounces treaties with other countries, appoints and recalls plenipotentiary representatives of the Soviet Union to foreign states, and receives the credentials and letters of recall of diplomatic representatives accredited to the Soviet Union by foreign states.

The Presidium of the Supreme Soviet of the U.S.S.R. institutes decorations (orders and medals) and titles of honour, military titles and other special titles; it awards orders and medals and confers titles of honour; it exercises the right of pardoning citizens who have been sentenced by judicial tribunals of the U.S.S.R.

Thus the Presidium of the Supreme Soviet of the U.S.S.R., by virtue of the powers granted to it, is the *highest permanently functioning organ of state power of the Soviet Union. It is elected by the Supreme Soviet of the U.S.S.R. and is accountable to it.*

In other countries there are no organs of power like the Presidium of the Supreme Soviet of the U.S.S.R. There a single person (president, king, etc.) heads the state.

Our state is headed not by a single person, but by a *collegium* consisting of 33 members of the Supreme Soviet of the U.S.S.R. who, to use Stalin's expression, constitute the "collegial president" of the U.S.S.R. This shows how consistently democratic, truly popular principles are applied in the organization of our higher organs of state.

* * *

The Supreme Soviet of each Union Republic elects from among its members a *Presidium* of its own, which is the highest permanently functioning organ of state power of the Republic and is accountable to its Supreme Soviet. The powers of the Presidium of the Supreme Soviet of a Union Republic, the number of its vice-presidents and the number of its members are determined by the Constitution of the Republic in question.

The Supreme Soviet of each Autonomous Republic likewise elects its own *Presidium*, the highest permanently functioning organ of state power of the Republic and accountable to its Supreme Soviet. The powers of the Presidium of the Supreme Soviet of the Autonomous Republic and its composition are set forth in its Constitution.

THE COUNCIL OF MINISTERS OF THE U.S.S.R.

Another permanently functioning higher organ of state power of the U.S.S.R. is one with which we are well acquainted through its decisions. This is the *Council of Ministers of the U.S.S.R.*, the name applied to the government of the Soviet Union.

The Council of Ministers of the U.S.S.R. is formed at a joint session of both Chambers of the Supreme Soviet of the

U.S.S.R. At the first session of the Supreme Soviet, held in March 1946, the government of the Soviet Union was formed in the following manner:

The head of the outgoing government, Comrade J. V. Stalin, submitted a written statement to the Chairman of the joint session of the Chambers declaring that the government surrendered its powers to the Supreme Soviet.

The Supreme Soviet accepted the statement of the government and unanimously commissioned Comrade Stalin to submit proposals for a new government. At the next joint sitting of the Chambers, the Chairman announced the composition of the new government as proposed by Comrade Stalin. After statements by Deputies the Chairman declared that there was no objection to any of the proposed candidates and that none of the Deputies insisted on a roll-call vote. The composition of the Council of Ministers of the U.S.S.R. as proposed by Comrade Stalin was then voted on as a whole and unanimously adopted amidst loud applause passing into an ovation in honour of *Comrade Stalin*, who was elected Chairman of the Council of Ministers of the U.S.S.R. and Minister of its Armed Forces. *V. M. Molotov*, Comrade Stalin's close associate, was approved as Minister of Foreign Affairs.

On March 3, 1947, the Presidium of the Supreme Soviet of the U.S.S.R. on Comrade Stalin's request released him from his duties as Minister of the Armed Forces of the U.S.S.R. because he was greatly overburdened by his principal duties.

The government of the U.S.S.R. is *responsible and accountable* to the Supreme Soviet which elected it. In the intervals between sessions, the government is responsible and accountable to the Presidium of the Supreme Soviet of the U.S.S.R.

The powers and composition of the Council of Ministers are set forth in the Constitution.

The Council of Ministers of the U.S.S.R. issues *decisions and orders* on the basis and in pursuance of the all-Union laws in operation, and verifies their execution. Its decisions and orders are binding throughout the territory of the Soviet Union.

The Council of Ministers of the U.S.S.R. is charged with such important duties as: the maintenance of public order; the protection of the interests of the state; the safeguarding of the rights of citizens; the fixing of the annual contingent of citizens to be called up for military service; the direction of the general organization of the armed forces of the Soviet Union; general guidance in the sphere of relations with foreign states.

Important powers are conferred upon the Council of Ministers of the U.S.S.R. relating to the management of the national economy. It takes the necessary measures for the carrying out of the state budget and the national-economic plans of the U.S.S.R., and also for the strengthening of the country's credit and monetary system.

The Council of Ministers of the U.S.S.R. co-ordinates and directs the work of the U.S.S.R. Ministries and other institutions under its jurisdiction.

The Ministries are the bodies in charge of the various branches of state administration and the national economy. Each minister is given sole authority to direct the branch of state administration entrusted to him and has a Collegium functioning under him. He issues *orders and instructions* pertaining to the said branch of administration.

The Ministries of the U.S.S.R. are divided into all-Union Ministries and Union-Republican Ministries. The all-Union Ministries direct the branches of the national economy which are of all-Union importance and require that they be administered from a single, all-Union centre. The Union-Republican

Ministries of the U.S.S.R. direct the branches of the national economy and state administration of all-Union importance which can be managed, and which it is advisable to manage, from the centre through corresponding Union-Republican Ministries of the various Union Republics. This system of Union-Republican Ministries makes it possible to combine the direction of any particular branch of the national economy or the state administration from the all-Union centre with the immediate direction of this branch by the corresponding Union-Republican Ministry of the Union Republic in question.

The Council of Ministers of the U.S.S.R. has the right, in respect of those branches of administration and economy which under the Constitution come within the jurisdiction of the U.S.S.R., to annul orders and instructions of Ministers of the U.S.S.R. and to suspend decisions and orders of the Councils of Ministers of the Union Republics.

Thus, the Council of Ministers of the U.S.S.R. is the *highest executive and administrative organ of state power of the Soviet Union, and is responsible and accountable to the Supreme Soviet of the U.S.S.R. and to its Presidium.*

The Soviet government differs fundamentally in its composition and functions from the government of old Russia and from all bourgeois governments.

In pre-revolutionary Russia political power and the administration of the country were by law vested solely in the tsar. In practice power was exercised, and the country was administered, by officials who acted in the name of the tsar. Arbitrary exercise of authority and violence practised against the people by government officials marked the savage rule of the old Russia. In all bourgeois countries political and administrative power is likewise concentrated in the hands of the powerful bureaucratic apparatus which stands above the people.

Of course nothing like this exists in our country today and its existence is entirely precluded. The government of the Soviet Union, as we have seen, enjoys exceedingly wide powers for the administration of the state and the direction of its affairs and of the entire life of the country. Its decisions and orders are binding throughout the Soviet Union.

At the same time the powers of the Council of Ministers of the U.S.S.R. are specified in the Constitution, the Fundamental Law of the land. All its actions must be based on all-Union laws and pursue the purpose of executing them. It is responsible and accountable for all its actions to the Supreme Soviet of the U.S.S.R. and its Presidium.

The Council of Ministers of the U.S.S.R. carries out the will of the peoples of the Soviet Union as expressed in the all-Union laws.

"Only here," said Comrade Stalin, "in the Land of the Soviets, does a government exist which stands solidly for the workers and collective-farm peasants, for all the working people of town and country...."

This explains why the Soviet government and its leaders headed by Comrade Stalin enjoy the full confidence and the unanimous support of all the people.

* * *

Each Union Republic has its *Council of Ministers*, which is the highest executive and administrative organ of state power of the Republic. The Council of Ministers of a Union Republic is appointed by its Supreme Soviet, is responsible and accountable to it and in the interval between sessions is responsible and accountable to the Presidium of the Supreme Soviet. The Union Republics have their own *Ministries*. They are divided into Union-Republican Ministries, of which we have already spoken, and Republican Ministries, which direct the branches of the national economy and state administration of Republican importance. The powers and the composition of the Council of Ministers of a Union Republic are defined by its Constitution.

Each Autonomous Republic likewise has its own *Council of Ministers*—the highest executive and administrative organ of state power of the Republic—and its own *Ministries*. The Council of Ministers of an Autonomous Republic is appointed by its Supreme Soviet, and its powers and composition are set forth in the Constitution of the Republic.

CHAPTER V.

THE COURTS AND THE PROCURATOR'S OFFICE

☆

THE OLD LANDLORD-BOURGEOIS COURTS

"COURTS and injustice go together"; "when a rich man goes to court he has nothing to worry about, when a poor man goes to court his very life is in doubt"; "judges and carpenters are alike, however they will their axe doth strike" —these proverbial sayings aptly describe the class character of the old landlord-bourgeois courts.

The very composition of the judiciary clearly proves whose interests the old courts were protecting. The "rural prefects," who were appointed by the governor of the province from among the landed nobility, held court over the peasants and punished them most cruelly. The Volost judges were appointed with the approval of the Zemstvo chief. These judges came from rich peasant families.

Up to the Revolution of 1905 the courts could order peasants to be flogged. The flogging of convicts as a means of punishment was practised down to the overthrow of the tsar in 1917.

To be eligible for the post of Justice of the Peace one had to own no less than 200 desyatins of land and in the cities real estate worth 3,000 to 15,000 rubles, depending upon the particular city. Moreover, judges had to be approved by the Senate, the highest judicial body. On this bench sat only members of the aristocracy and higher government officials. Sworn assessors were selected by a special commission, which consisted, among others, of the Marshal of the Nobility, the Procurator (public prosecutor) and the Zemstvo chiefs.

Cases charging offences against the tsarist system, that is, when revolutionaries were in the dock, were tried by so-called Judicial Chambers in which representatives of the upper social strata participated: the provincial Marshal of the Nobility, the head of the municipality (a capitalist) and the Volost elder (a kulak).

With a court so constituted it was no wonder that perfectly innocent people were often given severe sentences.

In capitalist countries the composition of the judiciary differs even today but little from that of the courts described above. The Supreme Court of the United States, for instance, consists of persons appointed for life by the President. Before their appointment most of the Supreme Court justices were legal advisers to the biggest corporations, in other words, were and still are loyal servants of capital. In the United States the federal and state Supreme Courts are authorized to interpret all laws and may declare them invalid.

The local judges in capitalist countries are completely under the influence of the various bourgeois parties. Bribery and corruption are so widespread among the judiciary that it is not at all a rare sight to see one of them removed from the bench to the prisoner's dock, for trafficking too openly in justice.

Particularly vicious is the persecution to which the bourgeoisie, with and without the agency of the courts, subjects revolutionary workers and farmers, Communists.

THE SOVIET COURTS AND THEIR FUNCTIONS

In our country the old, unjust system of administering justice was abolished by the Great October Socialist Revolution together with all the rest of the bourgeois machinery of state. Soviet power created a new, **a genuine** people's court.

The Soviet courts are **organs** *of the Soviet socialist state of workers and peasants.* In this regard, they radically differ from the courts in the capitalist countries, which act as organs of the dictatorship of the bourgeoisie, as instruments of judicial tyranny over the toiling masses.

Lenin and Stalin teach us that the Soviet state, the Soviet people, need the courts, first, to fight the enemies of Soviet government and, secondly, to fight for the consolidation of the new, Soviet system, to firmly anchor the new, socialist discipline among the working people.

Comrade Stalin demands the swift punishment of all violators of Soviet revolutionary law, whoever they may be, whatever position or office they may hold.

The Soviet courts are necessary likewise to settle disputes involving the rights and interests of Soviet citizens, government institutions and enterprises, collective farms and other public organizations.

On August 16, 1938 the Supreme Soviet of the U.S.S.R. adopted a new law on the organization of the courts. It defined the functions of the Soviet courts established under the Stalin Constitution.

First place was given by this law to the protection of the social and state system of the U.S.S.R.—the protection of public, socialist property, of socialist economy.

The verdicts and sentences of the Soviet courts mercilessly strike down the enemies of Socialism—the enemies of the people, traitors to the country, spies, saboteurs and wreckers.

In exposing the criminal activity of the enemies of the people, the Soviet courts teach the people unflagging revolutionary vigilance against agents of foreign powers who are being infiltrated into our country.

Since the victory of Socialism in the Soviet Union, the protection of public, socialist property has acquired particular importance. The Soviet courts severely punish embezzlers of state and co-operative or collective-farm property. Stern punishment is also meted out to speculators, bandits, rowdies, violators of labour and state discipline, and other offenders whose actions are detrimental to the interests of the state, the collective farms, and co-operative and other public organizations.

The decisions of the Soviet courts in civil cases protect the political, labour, housing, property, and other personal rights and interests guaranteed to citizens by the U.S.S.R. Constitution and the Constitutions of the Union and Autonomous Republics.

The Soviet courts defend the rights and interests of state institutions and enterprises, of collective farms, co-operatives and other public organizations.

It is a special feature of the Soviet courts that they not only punish criminals but set themselves the task of correcting them, of re-educating them. Soviet law inflicts no punishments that insult or degrade the dignity of man, as was the case under the tsar and still is the case in bourgeois countries. The Soviet state creates conditions which permit those serving their terms to atone for their guilt by honest labour and return to the ranks of full-fledged Soviet citizens.

In the Soviet Union capital punishment in peacetime was abolished by a decree of the Presidium of the Supreme Soviet of the U.S.S.R. dated May 26, 1947.

All the activities of the Soviet Courts are such as to instil in our citizens a spirit of strict and unswerving observance of

Soviet laws. They inculcate a sense of obligation to treat socialist property with care, to discharge duties to the state and the public honestly, in a spirit of devotion to the Soviet motherland and the cause of Communism.

SOVIET JUDICIAL ORGANS

The Soviet court is an organ of state that administers justice on the basis of the laws of our Soviet socialist state.

The system of courts in the Soviet Union is *uniform and equable for all citizens*, regardless of their nationality or race, their social origin, religion or their property and occupational status.

In our country justice is administered by various judicial organs. But the laws governing the organization of the courts and judicial procedure as well as the criminal and civil statutes of the Soviet Union are *uniform* throughout the country and *binding upon all courts*.

The basic Soviet judicial organ is the People's Court. The People's Courts try both criminal and civil cases. It is also the duty of the People's Courts to protect the electoral rights of Soviet citizens. Violations of labour discipline and disorderly-conduct cases are tried summarily by these courts. The higher courts hear and determine cases of major importance.

The Territorial, Regional and Area Courts and the Courts of the Autonomous Regions and National Areas have jurisdiction of criminal cases involving the security of the state, embezzlement of socialist property and other particularly grave offences; and of civil cases involving disputes between state or public organizations. Besides, these courts hear appeals from sentences and judgments of the People's Courts.

The Supreme Court of an Autonomous Republic is its highest judicial body. It is charged with the supervision of the judicial activities of all the courts of the Republic. It tries the criminal and civil cases of which it is given jurisdiction by law, and likewise hears appeals from sentences and judgments of the lower courts of the Republic.

The Supreme Court of a Union Republic is its highest judicial body. It is charged with the supervision of the judicial activities of all the other courts of the Union Republic and of the Autonomous Republics, Territories, Regions and Areas forming part of the Union Republic's territory. It tries criminal and civil cases of which it is given jurisdiction by law and hears appeals from sentences and judgments of the Territorial, Regional and other courts of the Republic.

The Supreme Court of the U.S.S.R. is the highest judicial organ of the Union of Soviet Socialist Republics. It is charged with the supervision of the activities of all the judicial organs of the U.S.S.R. and of the Union Republics. The Supreme Court of the U.S.S.R. is divided into five Collegiums: a criminal, a civil, a military, a railway and a water-transport Collegium. The President of the Supreme Court has the right to demand the record of any case in any court of the U.S.S.R. or of a Union Republic and to enter an appeal in the matter. The Supreme Court of the U.S.S.R. gives the courts guiding instructions on questions of court practice. It tries the most important criminal and civil cases, of which it is given jurisdiction under the law, and likewise hears appeals against the judgments and sentences of the Supreme Courts of the Union Republics as well as appeals against the judgments and sentences of the special courts of the U.S.S.R.

The Special Courts of the U.S.S.R.—military tribunals and Line Courts for the railway and water-transport systems—

are attached to the Soviet Army and Navy, and to the railway and water-transport services. The establishment of the special Military Courts arises from the necessity of strengthening the military might of the U.S.S.R. and military discipline. The special Line Courts are necessary because of the special conditions prevailing on the railways and in the water-transport system. During the Patriotic War the Line Courts were transformed into military tribunals.

THE ONLY GENUINE PEOPLE'S COURT IN THE WORLD

What are the principal distinguishing features of the Soviet court? How are cases tried in a Soviet court?

The Stalin Constitution has laid down the principle that *all judges are elective and subject to removal.*

All Soviet citizens entitled to vote are eligible for the judiciary.

Under the Stalin Constitution, the judges of the People's Courts are elected by the direct vote of the citizens of the respective districts by universal, equal and direct suffrage and secret ballot for a term of three years. Such a judge may be recalled by his constituents at any time for incompetence, and another elected in his place. The judges of the People's Courts are accountable to their constituents for their work and the work of the respective courts.

The court consists of a judge and two People's Assessors who have all the rights of judges when the court is sitting. Any citizen in possession of his electoral rights may be a People's Assessor. People's Assessors are elected and may be removed in the same manner as the judges of People's Courts. They each sit for only ten days a year and during this period receive their average earnings from their places of work. They are then relieved by other People's Assessors. In this way our courts are a sort of school for the training of the broad masses of the working people in state administration.

The Territorial, Regional and Area Courts and the Courts of the Autonomous Regions and National Areas are elected by the corresponding Soviets of Working People's Deputies for a term of five years.

The Supreme Courts of the Autonomous Republics and of the Union Republics are elected by the corresponding Supreme Soviets, likewise for a term of five years. The Supreme Court of the U.S.S.R. and the special courts of the U.S.S.R. are elected for a like term by the Supreme Soviet of the U.S.S.R.

The higher courts, just like the People's Courts, include two People's Assessors each, elected by the corresponding Soviets of Working People's Deputies or the Supreme Soviets.

Soviet judges are *independent and subject only to the law*. No organ of state power, whether of local or higher level, has the right to instruct a court how any case should be decided. Our judges are duty-bound to decide cases only according to Soviet law, which expresses the will of the Soviet people.

In all Soviet courts cases are tried *in public*. The parties concerned (the prosecutor, the accused, the plaintiff and the defendant) are heard in open court, the press being represented. The accused is also guaranteed the right to be defended by counsel.

Thus our courts hear and determine cases under the control of the Soviet public. Any citizen may enter a courtroom and be present during the trial of a case from beginning to end. Not infrequently trials are held in factories, mills or on collective farms to make possible the presence of a large number of persons closely interested in the decision of the case.

Such a system of court proceedings helps the masses to arrive at a clearer understanding of problems of state administration, the national economy, everyday life and morality. It cultivates in the masses a sense of socialist law, and induces them to combat crime.

Only in exceptional cases, specified by law, does the court sit behind closed doors. In these cases three judges occupy the bench, without any People's Assessors.

In all courts the proceedings are conducted in the language of the Union or Autonomous Republic or Autonomous Region where the court is held. Persons not knowing this language are entitled to acquaint themselves with the material of the case through an interpreter and to use their own language in court.

This procedure provides close contact between the courts and the population, makes each one of the numerous peoples of the Soviet Union feel the kinship between itself and the courts.

By virtue of all these specific features the Soviet courts are the only judicial tribunals in the world that may truly be called people's courts.

THE SOVIET PROCURATOR'S OFFICE

In old Russia the Procurator (Public Prosecutor) was called "the sovereign's eye." The highest officials holding this office were appointed by the tsar. The vast majority of procurators were selected from the nobility, which alone makes it quite clear whose interests the old procuratorship was defending.

In the capitalist countries Public Prosecutors are appointed from among the wealthy classes. In the United States, for instance, persons appointed government attorneys must furnish bond in the amount of 10,000 dollars.

In the capitalist countries it is the business of the Public Prosecutor to safeguard the interests of the bourgeois state and of the biggest capitalists. There he is the servant of capital.

In our country the Procurator's Offices *are organs of the Soviet socialist state of workers and peasants.* They differ therefore in every essential from the Public Prosecutor's offices in the bourgeois countries.

What is the function of the Soviet Procurator's Office?

There are cases when the acts or decisions of local organs of power or administration are at variance with the law, or when laws are incorrectly understood and applied. Then there are direct, deliberate violations of the law by official persons. It also happens occasionally that persons who are really enemies of the people worm their way into Soviet institutions and enterprises and make use of their official positions for the purpose of distorting the law and delaying its application, that is, commit sabotage against the Soviet state.

This made necessary the establishment of a special organ of state for the purpose of exercising supervisory power to ensure the correct application and strict execution of the law by all ministries and institutions subordinated to them, as well as by all officials and citizens of the U.S.S.R.

This organ is the *Soviet Procurator's Office*, originally established in the R.S.F.S.R. in 1922 and later on also in the other Soviet Republics. The Procurator's Office of the U.S.S.R. was formed on June 20, 1933.

The work of the Procurator's Office is intimately connected with the work of the courts. The Procurator's Office, like the courts, combats crimes committed against the Soviet state, fights against the enemies of Soviet power, against spies, saboteurs, wreckers and other agents of the bourgeoisie abroad. The Procurator's Office, like the courts, protects our public, socialist property, combats robbery, theft, economic mismanagement, bureaucracy, red tape, violations of labour and state discipline, etc.

The Soviet Procurator's Office also protects the personal rights of citizens. It safeguards the inviolability of the person: no person may be placed under arrest except by decision of a procurator (or a court).

The procurator has the right, and it is his duty, to appeal against all unlawful decisions and actions of state organs and officials. Every citizen is entitled to complain to the procurator concerning any violation of the law.

The Procurator's Office and the courts are confronted with common tasks but their methods of work are different.

The Procurator's Office institutes criminal proceedings and investigates criminal cases, ascertains the circumstances under which crimes were committed, collects evidence against the perpetrators of crimes and their accomplices, and sees to it that other investigating bodies act within the law. The courts try the cases submitted to them by the Procurator's Office, and the procurator maintains the prosecution before the court in the name of the Soviet state. At the end of the trial the court hands down its verdict and sentence. The procurator examines the decisions handed down by the courts as to their correctness, attends to the execution of the sentences and judgments of the courts and enters appeals in cases where in his opinion the sentence or judgment was erroneous.

The Soviet Procurator's Office stands guard over socialist legality. Like our courts it strengthens Soviet legality, Soviet socialist law and order.

The Procurator's Office is headed by the *Procurator-General of the U.S.S.R.*, appointed by the Supreme Soviet of the U.S.S.R. for a term of seven years. He exercises supreme supervisory power to ensure the correct application and strict observance of the law throughout the Soviet Union. The Procurator-General of the U.S.S.R. appoints the procurators of the Union Republics, the Autonomous Republics, the Territories, the Regions and the Autonomous Regions for terms of five years. Area, Regional and City Procurators are appointed by the procurators of the Union Republics, subject to confirmation by the Procurator-General of the U.S.S.R. and likewise for terms of five years.

Besides, the Procurator-General of the U.S.S.R. appoints the chief procurators in charge of the special organs of the Procurator's Office: military, railway and water-transport.

Why are procurators *appointed* and not elected?

The principal function of the Procurator's Office is to see that the laws are correctly and uniformly applied throughout the country. Soviet law must be *uniform* throughout the Soviet Union. This is demanded by the interests of the working people, no matter where they live, no matter to what nationality they belong.

In order to cope with this task successfully, procurators must be free to carry on their work independently of all local bodies whatsoever, must be subordinate only to the Procurator-General of the U.S.S.R. That is the reason why under our Constitution procurators are appointed centrally and not elected.

The appointment of procurators by a central authority does not in the least restrict the independence of the local authorities, because, unlike the executive and administrative organs of the Soviets, the procurator has no administrative powers.

Not he but the courts, elected directly by the people or by the Soviets, pronounce judgments and sentences.

In the performance of its work the Soviet Procurator's Office relies extensively on the assistance rendered by the Soviet public. Here the Soviet press plays an important part. Quite a few criminals and enemy agents have been detected with its aid.

The Procurator's Office, like the courts, is intimately connected with the masses, who see in it a protector of their interests and a defender of their dearly-loved, Soviet-ruled state.

CHAPTER VI

THE FUNDAMENTAL RIGHTS OF SOVIET CITIZENS

CITIZENS OF THE SOVIET UNION

THE YOUNGER generation, which has been reared and has grown up under Soviet rule, can hardly imagine how frightfully the people were deprived of civil and political rights under the tsar.

The very concept of "citizen" in our sense was unknown in tsarist Russia. It had no citizens; it had "subjects" of the Russian tsar, who were utterly dependent on the arbitrary will of the tsarist officials. The lot of the labouring masses and non-Russian nations was particularly hard.

The Soviet state in one of its first decrees, established the honourable appellation of *Citizen of the Russian Soviet Republic.*

With the formation of the U.S.S.R. a uniform citizenship for the entire Union was established for the citizens of the several Union Republics, and the words "Soviet citizen" acquired a still higher significance, denoting as they did not only membership of the first socialist state in the world but also fraternal alliance of the peoples that had formed it. Our poet V. V. Mayakovsky related how he presented abroad his "hammered-fast sickle-clasped Soviet Passport."

> Read this
> and envy;
> I'm a citizen
> of the Soviet Socialist Union!

The Stalin Constitution grants Soviet citizens rights and liberties that do not and cannot exist in any of the capitalist countries.

Moreover, our Constitution contains no restrictions limiting the rights it proclaims. Furthermore, the Stalin Constitution states in the same articles that set forth the rights of citizens how these rights are ensured in practice.

You will find nothing like it in the constitutions of the capitalist countries. They contain many reservations and restrictions of the rights of citizens set forth in their texts, while maintaining absolute silence as to the ways and means by which even these curtailed rights are to be given actual effect. Yet what counts most is, of course, the practical application of these rights.

The rights enjoyed by Soviet citizens under the Stalin Constitution are very great indeed. At the same time our Constitution imposes upon citizens definite duties to society and to the state. The duties of Soviet citizens correspond to the rights which they possess. Unlike the constitutions of the capitalist countries, the Soviet Constitution contains no duties without rights. The rights and duties of Soviet citizens are inseparable.

What are, then, the fundamental rights of Soviet citizens? How are these rights ensured in actual practice?

THE RIGHT TO WORK

Soviet youth does not know what unemployment is. Here is what Marshal of the Soviet Union K. E. Voroshilov once said on this topic at a meeting of the ranks of the Moscow garrison:

"I had occasion to experience personally what unemployment meant. It is something terrible. It affects you not only physically but morally. When a worker loses his job he feels that nobody wants him, though he is able-bodied and full of energy. He begins making the rounds of factories, mills and shops in search of employment and his job-hunting may continue for years; and if in addition he is a political suspect, he becomes altogether a pariah, an outcast of society, with nowhere to lay his head...."

Millions of workers and peasants used to scour Russia in search of work. In tsarist Russia there was no such thing as a right to work just as this right does not exist in any capitalist country even today.

In capitalist society there exists, on the other hand, the *right to the labour of others*. All persons of wealth enjoy this right by virtue of the fact that the factories and mills, the mines, the land, the forests and other means of production are their private property. The workers and poor farmers and peasants are compelled to work for these rich proprietors to earn a crust of bread.

The right to work will continue to be an unrealizable dream for all who toil as long as the capitalist system exists in their country.

Does anyone really suppose the capitalists operate their enterprises for the purpose of supplying the workers with work? Nothing of the kind. Every capitalist carries on his business for the sole purpose of making profit, of getting rich. When he sees that his business no longer yields him a profit, he closes down and throws the workers on the street.

In capitalist society there always is and will be a so-called reserve industrial army, the army of the unemployed. Its ranks are constantly swelling by the addition of farmers and peasants, handicraftsmen and artisans, reduced to ruin by the capitalists, landlords and kulaks. Others who join its ranks are the workers discharged from factories and mills as a result of the introduction of new and more efficient machinery, which makes it possible for the capitalists to employ a smaller number of workers.

And in times of economic crisis, when numerous factories close their doors and farmers reduce their crop areas, the reserve army of the unemployed increases several times over. Let us quote from some of the letters written by unemployed workers which the bourgeois author A. E. Johann* published in his story of the crisis in the United States in 1929-33:

McCormick, San Francisco, California:

"... I'm an old man and have long ago given up hope of ever finding work again.... I am old, starved, in rags and covered with lice. But let me tell you this much: I've been all over these parts during the last two weeks, from Frisco to San José and Point Reyes, and everywhere I came across sturdy young fellows willing to work who were just as down-and-out as I."

Charles Doyle, Phoenix, Arizona:

"I am a metal worker.... It is three years now that I was fired and I haven't found work since. The money I saved is eaten up long ago. Last night I slept in a shack on a wharf.... I have given up looking for work."

Harry Logan, Tucson, Arizona:

"I have been out of work for two years.... Every day about fifty people rummage around in the refuse, digging out anything edible they can find: bits of stale bread, cabbage leaves, scraps of meat and whatever else is digestible. But, of course, the garbage men, who have first choice, always pick the best for sale."

In capitalist society the working people experience increas-

---

* A. E. Johann, *Amerika. Untergang am Überfluss (America Succumbs to Superfluity),* Berlin 1932, pp. 164-66.—*Ed.*

ing poverty while the bourgeoisie is constantly growing richer. All bourgeois constitutions safeguard the right of private property in the means of production, the right of the possessing classes to exploit the labour of others.

In our country Soviet rule abolished the right of the former idle rich to live by the work of others.

The Stalin Constitution has granted all Soviet citizens the *right to work*. This means that each Soviet citizen has the right to guaranteed employment and payment for his work in accordance with its quantity and quality.

The right to work is one of the greatest achievements of the Soviet people. No such right exists or can exist in the capitalist countries. How is this right ensured in actual practice?

It is ensured by the socialist organization of our national economy, the steady growth of the productive forces of Soviet society, the elimination of the possibility of economic crises and the abolition of unemployment.

In our country the instruments and means of production have been taken away from the private owners and have been socialized, that is, turned into state or co-operative and collective-farm property. Thereby all citizens have been given access to the instruments and means of production, which makes guaranteed employment an actual possibility.

There are no exploiting classes in our country, and this means that all that part of the value created by labour which the capitalists, landlords and kulaks used to appropriate for themselves now remains at the disposal of all the working people, of the whole of our society. This alone has meant an immense improvement in the material conditions of the popular masses in our country.

And when we organized our whole economy on socialist lines, according to a plan, the material welfare and cultural level of the popular masses began to rise steadily, and was accompanied by a continuous expansion of our industrial and agricultural production. All this creates a constant rise in the demand for labour-power.

Thanks to the planned socialist organization of our national economy, the possibility of economic crises has been completely removed in our country. The introduction of perfected machinery and the improvement in production methods do not result here in depriving workers of their livelihood. The labour-power released is used by us to expand social production still more, to set up new plants and new branches of industry.

These are the conditions which make it perfectly possible for every Soviet citizen to implement his right to work. The people of the Soviet Union are never faced with the terrible threat of unemployment that forever haunts the workers in the capitalist countries.

Let us turn again to the United States. At the end of 1946 that country, according to American trade union statistics, already had over 5,000,000 people out of work. The bulk of them had been discharged from the various enterprises which had been busy fulfilling war orders or they had been demobilized from the army.

In our country, however, peacetime conversion did not entail the closing of any plants. Factories that had been producing for the national defence were converted to manufacture producer and consumer goods. The Supreme Soviet of the U.S.S.R. passed a law inaugurating a new five-year plan which envisages not only the rehabilitation of the national economy but its development to a point considerably above the pre-war level. The various governmental organs and the heads of enterprises and institutions are obliged by law to provide persons demobilized from the Soviet Army with work within the period of one month after their arrival at their former place of residence. They must also provide them with living accommodation, including heating. Those whose former dwellings, located in districts that suffered from enemy invasion, have to be rebuilt or repaired are given timber free of charge and loans in amounts of 5,000 to 10,000 rubles to be repaid within 5 to 10 years.

The toiling masses in the capitalist countries, who suffer from unemployment, starvation and poverty, realize the tremendous superiority of the Soviet socialist system over the capitalist system when they see how the right to work finds its practical application in the U.S.S.R.

THE RIGHT TO REST AND LEISURE

In the olden times conditions of work for factory hands and farm hands depended on the arbitrary will of the employer, and the same was true with regard to workers' rest and leisure. Factory owners made every effort to lengthen the working day and to lessen the number of days, hours and minutes of rest allowed the workers so as to wring the maximum of profit from their labour.

In tsarist Russia the workers had to fight hard to secure a shorter working day and rest from their onerous labour. They organized strikes and presented their bosses with their demands. The employers would suppress these strikes with the aid of the tsarist authorities, who resorted to the cruellest methods, including even armed force.

Nevertheless the workers compelled the tsarist government to issue a law in 1897 which prescribed a working day of 11 $1/2$ hours. But the same law allowed factory owners to resort to overtime work. Only the constant resistance and struggle of the workers forced the capitalist exploiters to keep their appetites within certain bounds.

Considering the long working day, the low wages paid and the undernourishment to which this led, the Sunday-rest was insufficient to restore the strength of the workers. Besides, there were almost no places where workers could spend their hours of rest and leisure in a cultured fashion. Here is the story told by an old Donets Basin miner, who worked in the Lidiyevka mine:

"The miners had no place to spend their Sundays. The clubs did not admit the likes of us. They were meant only for engineers and the better-paid office workers. We workers had to content ourselves with saloons and beershops. No decent entertainment was provided for the youth. The only pastime they could engage in was fisticuffs."

The workers never knew what it was to have an annual vacation. The only lengthy "vacation" they were acquainted with was unemployment, when they could "rest" under a bridge all they wanted.

This description fairly fits the condition of workers even today in capitalist countries.

Immediately it came into power the Soviet government established the eight-hour day, for which the workers had fought for decades. In some trades the hours of work were made shorter still.

On the tenth anniversary of the Great October Socialist Revolution the Soviet government shortened the working day to seven hours for the vast majority of workers. Those working underground or nights or engaged in particularly unhealthy work, as well as brain and juvenile workers (16-18 years old), were given a six-hour day.

From this it will be seen that as labour productivity increased the Soviet government shortened the working day in its effort to provide its citizens with a maximum of rest of leisure to engage in the arts and sciences and of time for general recreation.

The Stalin Constitution records the *right of Soviet citizens to rest and leisure* and immediately goes on to explain how this right is actually ensured.

It is ensured by the fact that in our country the working people of town and country themselves decide, through their higher organs of state power, and with the participation of their public organizations, how long their working day shall be and what rest and leisure they are to receive.

The Soviet citizen's right to rest and leisure is ensured by the fact that our country has the shortest working day in the world; by the fact that workers and other employees in addition to their weekly free day, are given annual vacations with full pay; by the fact that the working people are accorded the opportunity to rest in comfortable sanatoria and rest homes provided with cultural facilities.

All over the country the state and the trade unions have built numerous rest homes, sanatoria and clubs provided with cinemas, libraries and reading rooms, and have laid out stadiums, parks and athletic grounds. Big cities erect palaces of culture. Collective farms maintain their own rest homes, clubs and parks. Theatres, cinemas and museums may be found in all cities and towns and in many of the villages. All these establishments are open to the public either gratis or on payment of a small charge.

Tens of millions of Soviet citizens have been at these rest homes and sanatoria. In 1940, for instance, about 2,400,000 workers and other employees spent two-week vacations at rest homes. Over 1,600,000 workers were accommodated at weekend rest homes.

Then war broke out in Western Europe. In 1940 more

than half the population of the globe was already involved. The interests of our Soviet motherland demanded a lengthening of the working day, and a proposal to this effect was made by the All-Union Central Council of Trade Unions to the higher organs of Soviet power.

On June 26, 1940, the Presidium of the Supreme Soviet of the U.S.S.R. issued a decree lengthening the working day from seven to eight hours for wageworkers and from six to eight hours for office and juvenile workers. But workers employed in unhealthy occupations retained the six-hour day.

A few days after fascist Germany attacked the Soviet Union, on June 26, 1941, the Presidium of the Supreme Soviet of the U.S.S.R. authorized directors of factories and stores, on receipt of government permission, to introduce compulsory overtime work for a period of one to three hours a day, paying time and a half. The same decree abolished regular and supplementary vacations for the duration of the war, but compensation for unused vacations was retained.

It was clear to every Soviet patriot that these were absolutely correct and urgently necessary wartime measures.

The mobilization of all the forces of our people for the front, for victory, bore splendid fruit. When the war was over the pre-war working conditions and vacations were re-established at factory, office, mill and mine, and the system of monetary compensation for unused vacations was defined.

But the invasion of the Soviet Union by the German fascists had wrought immense destruction in the various branches of the national economy. Moreover, the war had delayed its normal development. Industry had been compelled to reduce considerably or even entirely stop the production of various machines, equipment, materials and other civilian goods required by the country. A considerable portion of the country's manpower, tractors, automobiles and horses had been diverted from the national economy to the army.

We must now work hard rapidly to restore the economic life of former enemy-invaded districts, to increase the output of industry and agriculture as much as possible, to raise the material welfare of the people far above the pre-war level, to strengthen still further the military and economic might of our country.

This is the reason why the Supreme Soviet of the U.S.S.R. at its session in February 1947 deemed it necessary to retain for the time being the eight-hour day for workers and other employees and to amend Article 119 of the Constitution accordingly. At the same time the Supreme Soviet of the U.S.S.R. decided to further amend Article 119 of the Constitution by adding the provision that for arduous trades the workday is reduced to seven or six hours, and to four hours in shops where conditions of work are particularly arduous, (of course, without reduction in pay). This clearly is a great relief for those engaged in such work.

The changes introduced in Article 119 of the Constitution leave *intact* the fundamental principle of the Constitution of the U.S.S.R. that citizens have the right to rest and leisure. This right is fully preserved by the conditions specified in this article of the Constitution and by our entire system.

The Soviet government and the trade unions are now releasing huge funds for the restoration of sanatoria and rest homes and the building of new ones. Wide range is given to the work of organizing cultural recreation of every description for the working people while on vacation.

It goes without saying that no capitalist country is or could be so solicitous about providing rest and leisure for the working people.

THE RIGHT TO MATERIAL SECURITY

M. I. Kalinin related the following incident concerning himself when he was working for a capitalist at a certain factory.

"I was a skilled worker and earned more than the average wage. Once I fell sick at work. I was ill for two months. Add to this the doctor's fees and the cost of the medicine and you will realize what position I, a skilled worker, was in. After two months of sickness I was 'clean broke,' as they used to say."

Such or a still sorrier fate awaited every worker in the old days in case he fell sick for any length of time.

When a worker lost his working capacity, he was of course discharged at once and no amount of pleading would do him any good—nobody cared a rap what became of an invalid.

And when old age came on, a worker whose toil had been enriching the capitalists for, say, 30 or 40 years, was shown the gate, thrown out on the street like a squeezed-out lemon.

Nor did the peasant masses have it any better. The vast majority of them lived from hand to mouth.

The peasant of old-time Russia lived in constant fear of the future. Crop failure or cattle disease, sickness, disablement or conscription into the army spelt ruin for his farm.

The same is true more or less to this day with regard to workers and poor farmers in the capitalist countries.

In 53 countries there is no state insurance for permanent disability. In 49 countries there is no state health insurance. In 41 countries there is no state old-age insurance.

And people age early in capitalist countries. At factory gates in the United States there sometimes hangs a sign: "Persons over 40 need not apply." When a worker has reached that age limit, it is very difficult for him to find employment. At rare intervals he may find odd jobs, but he is a doomed man.

In some capitalist countries working class pressure has forced the enactment of laws providing for some sort of state insurance of employees. But under these insurance systems the employees themselves must pay premiums from their meagre wages and the benefits paid out are insignificant.

For instance, in so rich a country as the United States the law provides that insured workers on reaching the age of 65 are entitled to a pension. However, for the vast majority this pension is only 15-20 per cent but not more than 30 per cent of their wages. About 10 million plant and office workers do not get even this miserable pension. Under this insurance system workers must contribute 2.5 per cent of their wages. In 1937-45 the plant and office workers of the United States paid over 3,000,000,000 dollars in insurance premiums but received only 550,000,000 dollars in pensions.

Organized workers receive some slight assistance from their Unions. Unorganized workers, however—and they form the vast majority—get no benefits whatever. When in need they are compelled to apply to public or private charity.

In our country, under Soviet rule, the situation is entirely different.

The Stalin Constitution records the *right* of Soviet citizens *to material security in old age, and also in case of sickness or disability.*

How is this right ensured?

By the fact that the Soviet state pays out of its own funds various pensions and benefits to workers and other employees; by the fact that the state supplies free medical aid at home. and in its clinics, dispensaries and hospitals; by the fact that a vast network of sanatoria is at the disposal of the people, a considerable part of the expenses being defrayed out of the state and trade union insurance funds.

Old age pensions are paid to workers and other employees (both men and women) for life, whether they are able to work or not, the amounts varying from 50 to 60 per cent of the pensioner's average earnings. The pension does not deprive the pensioner of his right to work. If the breadwinner dies, pensions are paid to the members of his family unable to work or under age.

Workers and other employees who have been permanently disabled as the result of an industrial accident, a professional disease, or in the discharge of their military duty receive pensions amounting from 50 to 100 per cent of their average earnings, while those who have lost their capacity to work from other causes receive pensions in the amount of one- to two-thirds of their average earnings.

In case of temporary disability, benefits amounting from 50 to 100 per cent of average earnings are paid.

Collective farmers, in their old age and in case of sickness or disability, receive material support from their collective farms as provided by their Rules.

Let us cite some figures indicating the care the Soviet state takes of the sick and the infirm. In tsarist Russia there were 93,000 hospital beds. In the Soviet Union there were 710,000 in 1940 and there are scheduled to be 950,000 in 1950. In 1940 the budget provided for the expenditure of 8,779,000,000 rubles on state insurance and social maintenance. The 1947 budget appropriated 29,900,000,000 rubles for these purposes.

These figures graphically illustrate the great and vital importance of the right of Soviet citizens to material security.

THE RIGHT TO EDUCATION

A peasant woman named Ananyeva was arrested once by the tsarist police for taking part in the revolutionary movement. She wrote in her depositions that it was the dream of her life to see her son go to high school. Tsar Alexander III on reading these depositions noted in the margin: "This is really horrifying—a muzhik trying to get into high school!"

In old Russia education was the special privilege, the exclusive right, of the wealthy classes. Ryabushinsky, one of old Russia's wealthiest manufacturers, openly expressed the contemptuous attitude of the bourgeoisie to workers' education in the following words:

"The workers are nothing but cattle. Teach them? Well, perhaps the three R's, so that they'll be of more use in the factory; but if they want anything else, they ought to be shot or hanged without mercy!"

The tsar's ministers prohibited the admission of the children of workers and peasants to secondary schools.

And, besides, where was a worker or toiling peasant to get the hundreds of rubles a year for tuition and maintenance in a secondary school, let alone an institution of higher learning?

In tsarist Russia more than three-fourths of the population were unable to read and write. Only isolated individuals were literate among the vast number of non-Russians. More than 40 nationalities had no alphabet.

In the capitalist countries a secondary or university education is beyond the dreams of the mass of the working people. In England, for instance, according to a statement by D. N. Pritt, M. P., only very few are fortunate enough to be able to study until they are 18 or 22 years old, and these fortunate ones are of course the children of the rich. To millions of children in these countries even the primary schools are closed. Take the United States. According to the Attorney General, there are millions of children who do not attend any school and more than 2,000,000 who go to schools that are absolutely unsatisfactory. 3,000,000 of the adult population of that country never received any schooling whatever, while 10,000,000 received so little schooling that they are virtually illiterate.

A wholly different state of affairs prevails in the Soviet socialist state of workers and peasants.

From its very inception the Soviet state made it its business to abolish that disgraceful inheritance from tsarism, illiteracy.

The Stalin Constitution granted all citizens *the right to education*. How is this right ensured?

The right to education is ensured to all citizens by an extensive system of primary, seven-year, secondary and special secondary schools and of higher educational institutions, in all of which instruction is conducted in the native language. It is further ensured by the organization in industrial and agricultural establishments of free vocational, technical and agronomic training, by night schools for young workers and peasants, one-year agricultural schools, and various study courses and correspondence schools.

The right to education is ensured furthermore by the fact that universal and compulsory elementary education and the seven-year school are free of charge, and by the payment of state stipends to students of higher educational establishments who excel in their studies. In the trade, railway and factory-apprentice schools, in the military, Suvorov and Nakhimov schools*

---

* *Suvorov and Nakhimov Schools.* Called after the great soldier, Suvorov, and Admiral Nakhimov, these schools were established during the Great Patriotic War. Pupils receive a secondary school education, and a knowledge of military subjects.

and in the special trade schools, the students receive at government expense not only tuition, but also full maintenance and dormitory accommodation if they are from out-of-town.

In 1940 the government found it necessary to make a small charge for tuition in the three senior classes of secondary schools and in the institutions of higher learning. But the bulk of the expenditure on tuition in these classes and in the higher schools is still borne by the state.

In February 1947 the Supreme Soviet of the U.S.S.R. approved of this change requiring the population to pay part of the cost of tuition, and amended Article 121 of the Constitution of the U.S.S.R. to this effect. This amendment, however, leaves *intact* the fundamental principle of the Stalin Constitution that citizens have the right to education, a right which is fully ensured by the conditions set forth in the said Article 121 and by the entire Soviet system.

Let us now see what have been the results of the constant concern of the Soviet state for popular education.

According to the general census taken on January 17, 1939, 18.8 per cent of the population of our country (mainly persons over 50) were still illiterate. Today this figure is of course much lower.

In tsarist Russia one out of every seventeen of the population attended school. In the U.S.S.R., the total number of children, adolescents and adults attending schools or taking courses was close to 48,000,000 during the school year 1938-39. That means that about one in four of the Soviet population is engaged in some form of study!

In tsarist Russia there were 91 institutions of higher learning with an aggregate attendance of 112,000. During the school year of 1946-47 we had about 800 institutions of higher learning, which were attended by 670,000 students, a figure far in excess of the combined student body of all Western Europe.

The words of the Stalin Constitution proclaiming the right of citizens to education read like an ode to education, science and culture.

THE EQUALITY OF MEN AND WOMEN

In pre-revolutionary Russia oppression weighed heavily upon the people, and particularly upon the women, who had to bear the additional yoke of enslavement to their husbands. Under tsarist law a woman was obliged to obey her husband in all things. If she left her husband he could have her brought back with the aid of the police. A woman had no right to take on a job without his permission. It was quite a common thing for husbands to beat and torture their wives. Among the eastern peoples a husband could even kill his wife and get off scott free. Women had no right to vote. They were greatly restricted in the part they could take in public life or public service, in the education they could receive, and even in the rights they had over their own property.

Worse still was the lot of the working women. They earned only half as much as men. In the countryside a woman had no earnings of her own. While unmarried she worked for her father; and after her marriage, for her husband. There were no laws to protect mother and child.

Besides working hard in factory or field, working women were worn out by exhausting and stupefying housework and the need to take care of their children.

The position of women in the capitalist countries differs little from what it was in old Russia. In most of the bourgeois countries women have no right to vote, or if they have it is greatly curtailed. Almost everywhere they are paid considerably less than the men for doing the same work as they. Few women hold responsible government positions even in those countries where the law allows this. Women suffer from many other disabilities. In some of the States of the U.S.A. the Statute Book still allows a husband deserted by his wife to have her brought back by the police. In the state of Arizona a woman is legally obliged to hand over the wages she earns to her husband. In the state of Alabama a husband has the legal right to correct a transgressing wife with a rod not exceeding two inches in thickness. Everywhere a woman who goes out to work remains a slave to the house. Especially hard is the lot of women in the Orient and in the colonies.

The Soviet state put an end to the outrageous inequality and oppression of women. It at once established complete equality of rights between men and women, something which does not exist in any capitalist country in the world.

Moreover, the Soviet state from its very inception began to take all the measures necessary to make the equality of men and women an actual fact. Lenin said that it was impossible to develop the revolution, to build socialist society, unless women were enlisted in economic, social and governmental work.

The Stalin Constitution has legally confirmed women's *equal rights with men in all spheres of governmental, economic, cultural, political and other public activity.*

In our country women have the same right as men to vote and be voted for in elections to any public office, even the highest. 277 women were elected to the Supreme Soviet of the U.S.S.R. in 1946 and more than 1,700 women to the Supreme Soviets of the Union and Autonomous Republics. 456,000 women are members of local Soviets.

Women have the same right as men to work, payment for work, rest and leisure, education and material security.

In the Soviet Union women may be found holding jobs which formerly were considered the exclusive preserve of men, such as, for instance, the job of foundryman, miner, blacksmith or drover. In our country women work as team (brigade) leaders, forewomen, locomotive engineers, shop superintendents and factory directors.

Formerly this had never been the case. Over 250,000 women are on the payrolls of our industrial establishments, working as engineers and technicians.

The collective-farm system has completely emancipated peasant women. In former times the work of a peasant woman was never appreciated in spite of all her drudgery on the farm; and all she earned was considered the property, first of her father and then of her husband. Today every woman working on a collective farm has her own workbook in which every item of work she does is carefully entered. This has made the collective-farm woman independent. Neither her husband nor her father can order her about as they used to.

950,000 women are in charge of collective-farm brigades and stock-breeding departments; 15,000 women function as collective-farm chairmen or vice-chairmen.

Women account for more than 43 per cent of the student body in our higher educational institutions, whereas in the capitalist countries of Western Europe they constitute less than 20 per cent. About 35,000 women work in research institutes; 200 women have been awarded Stalin prizes.

The role of women in the national economy assumed tremendous importance during the Patriotic War. In 1943, for instance, they performed almost three-fourths of the work done on the collective farms. Comrade Stalin said that the unexampled feats of labour performed by the women would go down in history.

During the war the women also took a direct part in the defence of the country by enlisting in the Soviet Army and the partisan detachments. About 120,000 women were awarded decorations, 62 of them being made Heroes of the Soviet Union.

The Soviet state displays great solicitude for the health of women and sees to it that they work under proper conditions. Female labour is forbidden in particularly hard work or in work injurious to health. Great attention is paid to the proper care of mother and child. Nursing mothers are not allowed to work at night or overtime. Special intermissions at work are allowed to mothers to feed their babies.

All state enterprises and institutions grant women special maternity leaves with full pay. Women are given additional assistance for nursing and taking care of their babies.

Under the Rules which every collective farm adopts for the management of its affairs, women are exempt from work for one month before and one month after childbirth, being credited during this period with half of their average number of labour days.

In the Soviet Union there is a vast network of institutions taking care of mother and child, a system unparalleled in any other country. In 1939 we had more than 5,300 special women's and children's medical consultation stations (of which there were only 9 in tsarist Russia). The same year we had over 140,000 maternity-home beds, 25,000 of which were in collective-farm maternity homes. (In tsarist Russia there were only a few thousand of such beds.) In 1940, 850,000 children were accommodated in our kindergartens and nurseries (as against a very few thousand in tsarist Russia); in 1950 the number accommodated is planned to reach the 1,250,000 mark.

In our country mothers of large families receive substantial benefits from the state to help them raise their children.

On July 8, 1944, that is, during the Patriotic War, the Presidium of the Supreme Soviet of the U.S.S.R. issued a decree providing for more extensive state assistance to expectant mothers, mothers of large families and unmarried mothers. Leaves before and after childbirth were lengthened from 63 to 77 days. The food rations of expectant mothers were doubled, beginning with the sixth month of pregnancy. The network of institutions serving mother and child was enlarged. Not only were state benefits to unmarried mothers provided for, but such mothers could entrust their children to the state to be fully maintained at its expense. Any such child, however, may be returned to its mother at her request to be brought up by her. Mothers now receive state benefits upon the birth of the third and every succeeding child. The honorary title of Heroine Mother is conferred on mothers who have borne and raised ten or more children. The following decorations are awarded to mothers of many children: the Heroine Mother Order, the Glory of Motherhood Order, and the Motherhood Medal.

Thus, as we see, women actually enjoy equal rights with men and the realization of these rights is ensured in actual practice.

THE EQUALITY OF CITIZENS OF ALL NATIONALITIES AND RACES

At a conference of collective-farm men and women of the Tajik and Turkmen Soviet Republics, Comrade Stalin said:

"In the old days, when the tsar, the capitalists and the landlords were in power in our country, it was the policy of the government to make one people—the Russian—the dominant people, and all the others—subject and oppressed peoples. That was a bestial, a wolfish policy."

The tsarist government incited the Russians against the Jews, the Tatars against the Armenians, the Armenians against the Tatars, etc. It organized special gangs, Black Hundreds, as they were called, consisting of such people as storekeepers, kulaks, landlords and policemen. These Black Hundreds made atrocious pogroms against the Jews, and beat up revolutionaries and democratically-minded students. By this policy the tsars, the landlords and the capitalists sought to fan the enmity between the various peoples of our country in order the more easily to rule and oppress the working people of all nationalities.

Even today the status of the various peoples in the bourgeois multinational states is largely reminiscent of the system that existed in the Russian Empire.

Let us take by way of illustration the status of the Negroes in the United States. Not only are their electoral rights restricted under various pretexts but many of those who are legally qualified are intimidated or forcibly prevented from voting. They are paid lower wages than White people. They must live in special quarters of the cities. They are not permitted to attend such public places as theatres, cinemas and restaurants on a basis of equality with the Whites. In "Jim Crow" states they may occupy in trains and street cars only the seats assigned to them. The children must attend special schools. Negroes, with rare exceptions, must get their college and university education at special institutions.

In February 1946 the owner of a store in the city of Columbia insulted the mother of a Negro named James Stevenson. When the latter took his mother's part, a mob of Whites tried to lynch him, but he made good his escape. Then the armed mob made its way into the Negro quarters of the city and with the aid of the police machine-gunned the Negro population. More than a hundred Negroes were arrested, and of these two were killed by the police. The upshot was that an all-White grand jury indicted the Negroes on a charge of "attempting to commit murder."

In capitalist countries inhabited by different nationalities there is no equality of nations. And even if the letter of the law provides for such equality, it does not exist in actual life. One nation is dominant while the others are dependent on or subject to it or are even persecuted by it. The colonial and semicolonial peoples of Asia, Africa and Indonesia suffer particularly from cruel national oppression on the part of foreign invaders.

The German fascists savagely pursued their policy of national and racial oppression in the countries they seized and in Germany itself.

How repugnant, how infinitely remote all this is from the realities of Soviet life!

From the very first the Soviet government pursued an altogether different national policy. On November 16, 1917, the Declaration of Rights of the Peoples of Russia, bearing the signatures of Lenin and Stalin, was published.

In it the Soviet government declared that it was inaugurating a policy of the voluntary and honourable alliance of peoples; that thenceforth there would be no dominant nation and no subject nations, but that all nations would be free and equal. Each people was granted the *right to decide for itself under what structure of state it wanted to live*, including the right to secede and form an independent state.

This Leninist-Stalinist national policy has been consistently carried into life by the Soviet government and the Bolshevik Party. Thanks to this policy national equality has been completely and consistently realized in our country. Due to this policy mutual confidence between the various peoples of the Soviet Union has grown up in place of the former mutual distrust, a confidence which has developed into indestructible friendship.

Equality of rights of Soviet citizens, irrespective of their nationality or race, in all spheres of governmental, economic, cultural, political and other public activity, has been inscribed in the Stalin Constitution.

No matter what nation or race a Soviet citizen may belong to, he enjoys the same political rights as all other citizens. He may be elected or appointed to any state office or post. He may work at any job he can cope with and receives equal pay for equal work. He may enter any educational institution and engage in any scientific or cultural work on an equal footing with all other citizens.

The Stalin Constitution most strictly prohibits any direct or indirect restriction of the rights of citizens on account of their race or nationality. It just as strictly forbids the establishment of any privileges whatever for citizens of any particular nation or race.

If any one in our country should conceive the idea of propagating such profoundly anti-Soviet views as that citizens of some particular nation or race possess exceptional qualities and should therefore enjoy special rights and privileges, or if anyone should manifest hatred or contempt for the members of any particular nation or race, he would soon enough find himself in the prisoner's dock. Any violation of the provision in the Constitution guaranteeing the equality of all citizens is punishable in our country as a grave political offence.

National equality, which has been completely realized in the U.S.S.R., is the watchword of the peoples who are fighting for their national liberation.

FREEDOM OF CONSCIENCE

Old Russia was a country of many different religions, from the Greek Orthodox faith to various heathen cults.

"Pre-eminent and dominant" among these was the Greek Orthodox faith. The Orthodox church enjoyed the special protection and support of the state. Its ministers were paid stipends by the state, which were in addition to the collections taken up among the members of their congregations. Attendance at bible classes was compulsory in all public and private schools. The school authorities saw to it that the school children attended divine service and performed religious rites. Adults in employ who were remiss in their religious worship faced the threat of discharge.

Birth, marriage and death certificates were issued by the church authorities. A marriage concluded without a religious ceremony was considered illegal. The offspring of such a marriage was deemed illegitimate and did not enjoy the protection afforded to children born in wedlock.

People who professed a non-Orthodox religion were limited in their rights and frequently suffered cruel persecution. Antireligious propaganda was forbidden and punished as a crime. For instance, K. A. Timiryazev was discharged "because of his godlessness" from the Petrovsky Agricultural Academy, which today bears his name.

Clearly, freedom of conscience was out of the question in such conditions.

By decree of February 3, 1918, the Soviet government proclaimed freedom of conscience and abolished all religious restrictions. The decree states:

"A citizen may practise any religion he chooses or none at all."

This is what *freedom of conscience* means. To ensure it in

practice the Soviet government in the same decree *separated the church from the state and the school from the church.* This means that the church and the clergy are deprived of state support and the clergy is forbidden to teach religion in the schools. Birth, marriage and death certificates are now issued by the civil authorities, the Soviets.

The same decree, however, ensured the free exercise of religious rites and ceremonies. Places of worship and objects of religious ceremony were assigned to the respective religious congregations for their use free of charge.

This law is in full force and effect to this day. The attitude of the Soviet state to religion, to believers and their organizations is defined as heretofore by this law, incorporated in the Stalin Constitution.

The Stalin Constitution guarantees Soviet citizens genuine freedom of conscience. It assures their right to the free performance of religious rites and ceremonies. At the same time the Constitution also guarantees the right to engage freely in antireligious propaganda.

Soviet government is conducted on scientific principles. The Soviet authorities do all in their power to promote the enlightenment of the popular masses. They help them in every way to acquire a knowledge of the sciences, acquaint them with the scientific explanations of the phenomena of nature and of human society, introduce them to a knowledge of the origin of the world and of man, and of the origin and significance of religion throughout the history of man. The youth are taught in the Soviet schools the eternal nature of matter, the evolution of plants and animals, the changes effected in social and political systems by means of the class struggle and revolution. The Soviet state and the Communist Party are raising a young generation of brave young men and women, free from all prejudice, who believe only in their own strength and in the collective potency of the working people—are raising a generation of conscious builders and fighters for a happy life on Soviet soil, for Communism.

The Soviet state protects *all its citizens* alike, irrespective of their religious persuasions and their attitude toward religion. It not only takes no action against those who believe that a supernatural power governs the destinies of people, but protects them from all religious persecution.

The German fascists in the foreign countries and Soviet districts occupied by them harassed believers, mocked their religious sentiments, looted, defiled and destroyed churches and murdered ministers of religion. The Soviet government exposed these crimes at the time and declared that those guilty of them would be punished with all the severity of the Soviet laws. It included a representative of the Orthodox Church in the Extraordinary State Commission for the establishment and investigation of the atrocities committed by the Nazi invaders.

Special government organs have been set up to deal with affairs concerning religious worship. It is the main object of these organs to supervise the correct and prompt execution of the laws and decisions of the Soviet state pertaining to the activity of religious congregations without, however, interfering in any way in their internal affairs.

The policy of the Soviet government in the question of freedom of conscience has won the appreciation and support of believers and clergymen of all denominations in our country as well as abroad.

POLITICAL LIBERTIES

Under the tsar there were special officials who saw to it that no "free thought" got into the press. Not one book, not one issue of a newspaper could be published without their sanction.

Everywhere the tsarist censors discovered "free thinking" and an endeavour to overthrow the absolute monarchy. Thus, for instance, one of these officials deleted in a cook book a phrase containing the words "free spirit" (in archaic Russian), though a heated oven with a "free air" supply was meant, inasmuch as in his opinion it suggested revolution. Another such numskull struck out in a hymnal a passage stating that the Holy Virgin was "invisibly subduing cruel, beast-like tyrants" as a possible allusion to the tsar.

These examples, which sound like jokes to us, show the position of the press under tsarist rule. Revolutionists were compelled to set up their own printing presses underground, and publish and distribute their literature in secret, as was done at the time by Comrade Stalin in the Caucasus. The central and leading newspaper of the Bolsheviks was published abroad and smuggled into and secretly distributed in Russia.

The police and special agents of the *"Okhrana"* (tsarist secret police) carefully watched all subjects of the tsar and arrested anyone who uttered an incautious word. Meetings were prohibited. Street processions and demonstrations were mercilessly broken up by force of arms, as for instance the demonstrations organized by Comrade Stalin in Tiflis and Batum. Participation in secret societies made one liable to arrest, imprisonment, exile and even capital punishment. Tens of thousands of Bolsheviks and other revolutionists landed in jail, served sentences of hard labour or lost their lives in the battle for freedom.

The Great October Socialist Revolution destroyed the power of the landlords and capitalists, set up a new, Soviet state system, which guaranteed the working people all political rights and liberties.

The Stalin Constitution guarantees the following *political rights* to all citizens: freedom of speech, freedom of the press, freedom of assembly, including the holding of mass meetings, street processions and demonstrations.

The Stalin Constitution ensures the citizens of the U.S.S.R. the *right of association,* that is, the right to form public organizations such as trade unions, co-operative societies, youth, sports and defence organizations, cultural, technical and scientific societies and the Communist Party.

The Stalin Constitution guarantees citizens *inviolability of the person and home, as well as privacy of correspondence.* No one in the Soviet Union may be arrested except by decision of a court or with the sanction of a procurator. Representatives of government authorities may enter the home of a citizen without his permission only in cases specified by law. Similarly, the personal correspondence of a citizen may be examined only with the permission of a procurator when such examination is necessary to discover the author of a crime.

What actually ensures these political rights and liberties in our country?

They are ensured by our entire social and state system.

In our country state power is in the hands of the working people. The Soviet state, being truly a state where power is in the hands of the people, is not interested in the least in curbing political rights and liberties. On the contrary, the Soviet state is directly interested in having the political and social initiative of the popular masses develop as widely as possible until it embraces the entire citizenry. Precisely these are the aims and objects of the political rights and liberties proclaimed in the interests of the working people by the Stalin Constitution.

In our country, the working people have at their disposal all the material means requisite for the realization of their political rights and liberties. The working people and their organizations can make unhindered use of the printing presses, stocks of paper for the printing of newspapers and books, of the premises required for holding public meetings, of broadcasting stations, communications, etc.

That explains why in the Soviet Union civil liberty is not a mere phrase. It is an actual fact, part and parcel of our life. Almost all workers by hand and brain and almost all peasants in our country belong to public organizations. Tens of millions of people are members of our various voluntary societies. Our social and state system ensures all of these societies every possibility of development and prosperity.

The social and political life of the labouring classes in the capitalist countries lacks the freedom, range and vigour characteristic of our country. There can be no similarity. It is the bourgeoisie which holds sway there. The only right which bourgeois constitutions guarantee without reservation is the right of private ownership of the means of production. All other rights the bourgeoisie recognizes only in so far as they subserve this underlying right. Equality of rights means exclusively the formal equality before the law established by the bourgeoisie. Legal equality does not, however, in the least do away with actual economic inequality, the class inequality that exists in capitalist society. On the contrary, it is this very inequality that the exploiting capitalist system depends upon. As a matter of fact, political rights and liberties are enjoyed in the main by the wealthy classes, who form the insignificant minority.

Judge for yourselves. How can one talk of freedom of speech, of the press or of assembly for workers, poor farmers and peasants when the printing presses, stocks of paper, the radio stations and meeting halls are the private property of the capitalists? No owner of a newspaper will allow the publication of any article or news item that does not meet with his approval. No radio company will allow any announcer to broadcast anything its owner does not want him to. All the most desirable premises for public meetings belong to capitalists, and the rent they demand for them is exorbitant, not to mention the fact that the owners of these premises may refuse to rent them altogether.

Or let us take the right to organize. In capitalist society the working people are so heavily exploited that for this reason alone it is exceedingly difficult for them to exercise their right to organize. This explains why in capitalist countries only a small minority of the working people belong to unions. Moreover, their unions are under constant attack by the bourgeois authorities who harass them in every way.

The political and other rights of the working people are restricted and trampled underfoot not only in countries like Spain, Portugal, Greece, Turkey, Brazil and Chile but also in countries like the United States which vaunt their democratic liberties. There the Taft-Hartley Act, passed in 1947, restricts the rights of trade unions in collective bargaining between management and labour, forbids the unions to demand closed shops, limits the right of plant and office workers to strike and prescribes that trade unions which desire to be legally recognized must remove Communists from their leaderships, etc. The entire working class violently opposed the bill, yet it was passed by both houses.

In the light of such facts it becomes perfectly clear how right Comrade Stalin was when he said:

"Real liberty can exist only where exploitation has been abolished, where there is no oppression of some by others, where there is no unemployment and poverty, where a man is not haunted by the fear of being tomorrow deprived of work, of home and of bread. Only in such a society is real, and not paper, personal and every other liberty possible."

CHAPTER VII

THE FUNDAMENTAL DUTIES OF SOVIET CITIZENS

ON RIGHTS AND DUTIES

INQUIRE among the members of the older generation, among comrades who lived and worked in pre-revolutionary Russia, what their attitude was towards the duties which the state imposed upon them or the laws issued by the tsarist government.

They will no doubt reply:

"We tried to shirk these duties and evade the tsarist laws."

This is quite comprehensible, for the landlords and capitalists were the lords and masters of old Russia. They established their own system of society so odious to the working people.

Rights and duties they apportioned as follows: rights for the bourgeoisie, duties for the toilers. Take, for instance, work. Whose duty was it to work? Exclusively the duty of the classes possessed of little or no property at all, that is, the worker and peasant masses. And whose was the right to enjoy the fruits of labour, all the good things in life? That was the right of the rich, the exploiting classes, that is, the capitalists, landlords and kulaks.

No wonder the working people strove to shirk the duties imposed upon them by the bourgeois state, and to evade the laws issued by a government alien to their interests. The workers and peasants strove to overthrow the rule of the bourgeoisie and set up the rule of the working people.

Under Soviet rule the working people became the masters of their own country and set up their own order of things.

With us there are no rights without duties, just as there are no duties without rights. Take the question of work. Who in our country is obliged to work? *Everybody.* The Stalin Constitution declares that work "is a duty and a matter of honour for every able-bodied citizen." At the same time the Constitution grants all Soviet citizens the right to receive the products of labour in accordance with the quantity and quality of work done by each. On the other hand, those who do not work though able to work are deprived by our Constitution of the right to receive the products of work: "He who does not work, neither shall he eat."

Being complete masters of their country, the working people have themselves established the rights and duties of Soviet citizens. Each one of these duties fully accords with the vital interests of the working people. In the U.S.S.R. there is no conflict between the interests of the working people and those of the state, of society. The interests of both coincide completely.

We have established a just social and state system. We want to consolidate and further develop it. We are ready to defend this system, to defend our Soviet motherland with all our strength. What is required to accomplish this purpose?

This requires, primarily, that every Soviet citizen honestly discharge the duties set forth in Articles 130 to 133 of the Stalin Constitution.

What are these duties?

TO ABIDE BY THE STALIN CONSTITUTION, TO OBSERVE THE SOVIET LAWS

The Stalin Constitution expounds the principles of our social and state system. It legally enacts an order under which exploitation, the oppression of some by others, is impossible, an order under which power is in the hands of the working people. Strict observance of the Constitution ensures the prosperity and might of our country and hence the personal welfare of Soviet citizens.

That is why the first commandment addressed to the Soviet citizen is—*faithfully to abide by the Constitution of the Soviet Union* as well as the Constitution of your Union Republic.

The Stalin Constitution is our law of laws. All other laws are shaped in conformance to it. There is a fundamental difference between Soviet laws and the laws of capitalist countries.

There the political power under which the laws are issued is in the hands of the bourgeoisie. There the laws are an expression of the will of the ruling exploiting classes. The bourgeoisie attempts to justify its laws by claiming that they are passed in the interests of the whole of society. But this is a lie and a deception. What common interests can there be between capitalists and workers, between big landowners and small farmers, between exploiters and exploited, between the sated and the starved? In capitalist society there is a profound and irreconcilable conflict between the interests of the working people, on the one hand, and those of the ruling classes, on the other. What is advantageous to the bourgeoisie is disadvantageous to the working people and vice versa.

Such a conflict of interests does not and cannot exist in Soviet socialist society.

Our laws reflect the will of the people. They record what the representatives of the people have deemed right and necessary to carry into life in the interest of all society, that is, of all toilers, the only ones who make up our society.

The Soviet socialist state represents, expresses and defends the interests of the whole people. The interests of the Soviet state, of Soviet society, and the interests of the people coincide. They are identical, inseparable.

This is the reason why Soviet laws must be observed without fail, in the interest of strengthening the Soviet state, the Soviet socialist system, and consequently, also in the interest of the personal welfare of Soviet citizens.

He who fails to observe, who violates Soviet laws acts contrary to the will of the people, harms the interests of the Soviet state, of Soviet society. Violations of Soviet law are punished by the courts in accordance with the gravity of the offence and the culprit's degree of guilt.

Anyone who is guilty of even a slight evasion of any law, decision or order of the Soviet state wittingly or unwittingly affords assistance to the enemies of the Soviet motherland.

Strict, unreserved observance of the law is the second commandment addressed to the Soviet citizen.

TO MAINTAIN LABOUR DISCIPLINE

In days gone by there were cases when a new labour recruit at a factory would work for all he was worth; but his fellow workers would soon cool his ardour with the question:

"What's the rush? Want to make the boss rich quick?"

Indeed, being industrious in a capitalist enterprise only enhanced the profits of the employer while yielding no tangible advantage to the worker. However hard he tried he always remained stuck in the mire of poverty.

The organization of labour in a capitalist-owned establishment was maintained chiefly by the *discipline of prospective starvation*: the worker was afraid that if he worked badly he would be dismissed and reduced to starvation.

All this changed radically under Soviet rule. Economic enterprises now belong in this country either to the state, collective farms or co-operatives. The more diligently a worker or collective farmer works—the richer our country, our society consisting only of working people, the more prosperous the collective farms, the greater everyone's share for his labour, the better supplied are the workers and collective farmers. The working people have become their own masters, they work for their common benefit, and therefore have an interest in working to the best of their ability.

This explains why the organization of labour in our socialist enterprises is based on the free, conscious discipline of the workers themselves.

Without such free, conscious discipline, *socialist emulation* aiming at the fulfilment and overfulfilment of production quotas in the shortest period of time would be impossible in our enterprises, just as the Stakhanovite movement would be impossible. The Stakhanovites are our foremost workers and peasants who have mastered the technique of their work. They have invented and continue to invent each day a multitude of improvements and technical innovations which raise the productivity of labour. Every enterprise has its "two hundred percenters," "three hundred percenters," and even "thousand percenters," that is, Stakhanovites whose output is double, treble or tenfold the specified quota. They serve as examples of efficiency to their fellows.

Work based on the discipline of those who perform it, a

discipline exercised freely and consciously, cannot even be conceived of in capitalist society where people do not work for themselves but for exploiters.

Such discipline is strengthened by the very nature of the collective work in the public, socialist enterprises, where the management comes from the working people and each worker is paid according to the quantity and quality of the work he performs.

Those who particularly distinguish themselves at work receive premiums or are awarded testimonials, badges or decorations. The highest title awarded for distinguished work is that of *Hero of Socialist Labour*. It is conferred, together with the Order of Lenin and a gold Hammer and Sickle Medal, for exceptional services in facilitating the advancement of the national economy, culture or science, or enhancing the power and fame of the Soviet Union.

The list of Heroes of Socialist Labour includes the most prominent statesmen, business executives, designers and scientists as well as rank-and-file workers and collective farmers.

Payment for work according to quantity and quality of performance and the especial awards for proficiency are most important means of raising the sense of responsibility of the working people. Such payment and awards encourage them to work conscientiously and in disciplined fashion for the fulfilment and overfulfilment of the tasks assigned them.

Parallel with these measures other means of improving labour discipline must be employed.

The vast majority of Soviet citizens understand that now they work for themselves, and therefore they have changed their attitude toward labour: they work honestly, and conscientiously maintain labour discipline. However, among the popular masses there are still politically backward people who have not yet abandoned their old views on work, the views working people held when they were still drudging like convicts for the capitalists and landlords. There are still people among us who try to shirk work, to give society as little as possible but take from it as much as possible. To such people coercion must be applied.

While passing laws and regulations prescribing coercive measures, the Soviet government and the Communist Party of the Soviet Union at the same time carry on constant propaganda among the masses, explaining the necessity of such measures for society, the Soviet state, the working people themselves.

Quotas of output and rates of payment for work are fixed in our state enterprises and institutions in agreement with the trade unions. If any worker continually fails to fulfil the assigned quota of work he may be transferred to a lower category. If the quality of work done is not satisfactory, either less than the standard rate is paid or the work is not paid for at all.

Absence from work without a legitimate excuse, that is, absenteeism, is punishable as a criminal offence and any worker or other employee found guilty of it by a People's Court may be sentenced to a term not exceeding six months, the term to be served by the offender continuing to work on his job and suffering a deduction from his pay of not more than 25 per cent. Quitting one's job without authorization is punishable, upon conviction by a People's Court, by imprisonment for a period of from two to four months.

Factory directors, chief engineers and the chiefs of goods testing departments who release goods of bad quality or goods which do not conform to specifications are liable to prosecution for crimes considered equivalent to sabotage.

Such strict discipline is enforced on demand of the workers themselves, who have no desire to tolerate in their midst any loafers, absentees, producers of waste and persons flitting from job to job.

In the collective farms every able-bodied member is obliged to do enough work in the course of each year to amount to a fixed minimum of labour days. The collective farm rules prescribe the following punishments for those who violate labour discipline or work badly: a warning, a reprimand or reproof at a general meeting, a fine equivalent to no more than five labour days, suspension from one's position, and the like. People who fail to reform are expelled from the collective farm, if a general meeting of the collective-farm members so decides.

In Soviet socialist society the strict observance of labour discipline is of paramount importance.

In pre-revolutionary times, when anybody violated labour discipline in any factory or shop, its owner was the only one who suffered. His profits were touched and that was all. But our socialist economy is conducted according to a uniform national plan. Here advance estimates are made of what products each separate establishment must produce, how much of each and in what periods of time, in order to permit the national economy as a whole to work smoothly and without interruption and thus supply the country with all it needs. Clearly, in the U.S.S.R. any violation of labour discipline, even if confined to a few establishments, inevitably leads to a disruption of the normal working of our national economy, occasioning a direct loss to the entire country.

The strict and steadfast observance of labour discipline is the third commandment addressed to the Soviet citizen.

HONESTLY TO PERFORM PUBLIC DUTIES

L. Nikulin, a Soviet writer, relates the following incident in his *Southern Urals.*

A train pulling a heavy load of tanks and shells was chugging along in the direction of the front. Signal boxes and small stations flashed by in quick succession. Suddenly the train ground to a stop in the middle of the steppe.

"What's the trouble here?" asked Senior Sergeant Rodionov, running up to the engine.

"The rear control plug has a leak in its thread and the boiler might explode," replied the locomotive engineer. "We'll just about manage to make the next depot. And yet it's a mere trifle. All you have to do is tighten up on the plug. But then, of course, you'd have to extinguish the fire in the engine. That'll put her out of commission for a whole day. But we can't afford that. With the load she's pulling every minute counts."

He stepped up to the firebox and opened the door. A fierce blaze was raging in the grate. Suddenly the engineer, looking strangely at his assistant, exclaimed:

"Open up everything! Let her have air! Come on, let's have a draft." And after a while:

"Now lay on coal!"

The bright red flames gradually grew dim under the thickening layer of coal which was discharging poisonous fumes beneath, while above the boiler roared under a pressure of ten atmospheres.

"Look here now," said the engineer, huskily. "Don't fall asleep on this job. If anything should happen just pull me back."

With these words he disappeared in the stifling heat of the gaping black firebox.

Followed long moments of anguished waiting. Rodionov, who had seen death dozens of times, and who himself had once been almost burned to a cinder in his tank, felt beads of perspiration trickle down his back between his shoulder blades.

At last a sombre jack-knifed silhouette could be discerned in the firebox. The engineer almost fell into Rodionov's arms. His face was haggard and pitch-black with soot. He greedily inhaled deep, long breaths of the cold raw air and said:

"She's ... ready now ... let's go!"

"Say you, engineer!" Rodionov called, breathing hard with emotion.

The latter looked at him in silence.

"What's your name, comrade?"

"Chernikhov."

"What Depot?"

"Troitsky. Why do you ask?"

"Nothing. You sure are a fine bunch, you people from the Urals!"

He embraced the engineer and jumped off the steps of the engine.

The buffers clanged and soon the train was gathering speed.

What impelled Chernikhov to act so selflessly?

He was impelled to act in this way because he was *keenly conscious of his duty to society*. He was conscious of the fact that the interests of the workers, of toiling folk like himself, the interests of all Soviet society—the interests of the country of which the working people themselves are the masters required such action of him. He felt his kinship with all society, with the whole of his country, and for its sake he risked his life.

Such profound consciousness of public duty was, of course, something impossible in old Russia nor does it exist today in any capitalist country, where society is divided into mutually antagonistic classes pursuing opposite interests.

The public duty of a Soviet citizen demands first and foremost honest compliance with the laws ordained by the Soviet state. In the U.S.S.R. the law expresses what the finest representatives of society chosen by the entire people have recognized as necessary and *obligatory* in the interests of the whole of society. Once the Soviet citizen has become cognizant of the demands of the law, they become injunctions proceeding from his sense of public duty, and he abides by them not from fear of punishment but voluntarily, because he realizes the necessity of such compliance in the interest of society, of his country.

The most progressive, the socially most conscious section of the Soviet citizenry conceive public duty to be something broader than the direct mandates of the law. They understand public duty to comprise all that may be necessary and useful to consolidate and develop socialist society, that may advance the welfare of the land of Soviets.

For example, the service rules and regulations demanded of engineer Chernikhov that on discovering the defective condition of the locomotive he should bring it, using every precaution, to the nearest depot and turn it over for repairs. But then the train would have arrived at the front a whole day late. His high sense of duty as a Soviet citizen prompted him to adopt a different course, albeit at the risk of his life.

Soviet law requires that everyone fulfil the required standard of output. The foremost workers and collective farmers, the Stakhanovites, not only fulfil but overfulfil several times the quotas which they are set. Time and again a brigade assigned a rush job will not leave the shop for days on end so as to finish ahead of schedule.

In the minds of the politically-advanced Soviet citizens public duty requires that everyone promote the commonweal with all his heart and soul, that everyone place the interests of the public above his own personal interests, that he combat whatever is of harm to socialist society, to the country. The socially-minded Soviet citizen, on noticing that something in his factory or collective farm is not as it should be, will not wait until the matter is straightened out but will take a hand himself. When a Stakhanovite sees that some of the workers do not fulfil their quota, he does what he can to help his lagging comrades, to impart to them his experience and thus achieve a *general increase* in labour productivity. A public-spirited Soviet citizen will not allow a single instance of a dishonest, let alone outright criminal, attitude to one's duties to go by without rousing public opinion against such delinquency.

TO RESPECT THE RULES OF SOCIALIST INTERCOURSE

When the Constitution refers to socialist intercourse it has in mind the whole of our country, the whole of our socialist society, and concerns those rules of conduct which Soviet citizens should observe in relation to society and to each other.

Every human society has, of course, rules of social intercourse. The fundamental rules governing the conduct of people are recorded in the laws of each country. A violation of these rules constitutes a criminal offence and is punishable as such. Besides, in each society there are rules of conduct which are not recorded in laws. Although a violation of them entails no legal punishment, it is condemned by the public opinion prevailing in the country in question. The rules of human conduct are called morality.

The substance of a country's morality, of its rules of social intercourse, depends upon its social system. Whatever the social system is, such are the rules of social intercourse.

The social system of pre-revolutionary Russia was based on *private property* in the means of production. Private property made it possible for some people to exploit others. The old society, Lenin said, was based on the idea that either you rob the other fellow or he robs you, either you work for somebody else or he works for you. Private ownership *disunited* people, introduced distrust, enmity and strife among them.

Needless to say, the rules of social intercourse in bourgeois society permit and justify the exploitation of man by man, and all relations between people that logically follow therefrom. One of the principal rules of bourgeois social intercourse is, for instance, the inviolabity of private property in the means of production, which has been embodied in the Constitutions and laws of all capitalist countries. The whole life of bourgeois society is steeped in the profit motive, is dedicated to personal enrichment. Bourgeois morality finds clear expression in such sayings as "every man for himself and the devil take the hindmost"; "everyone loves himself best"; "after us the deluge."

All these rules of social intercourse have lost their validity in our country since public, socialist ownership of the instruments and means of production became the foundation of our social system. Public, socialist ownership *unites* people on the basis of joint labour in public enterprises, and promotes confidence, friendship and comradeship between them.

This is the soil upon which entirely different rules of social intercourse, the direct opposite of the rules prevailing in bourgeois society, have come into existence in our country and are progressively penetrating the minds of all its citizens.

Among the fundamental rules governing the life of Soviet socialist society we have, for instance, the duty of all its able-bodied members to work, the impermissibility of one man exploiting another, and the inviolability of public, socialist property. These and other rules of social intercourse under Socialism are embodied in the Constitution of the U.S.S.R. and in our laws. The Constitution directs the life and conduct of the millions upon millions of Soviet citizens. The Constitution of the U.S.S.R. is, as M. I. Kalinin expressed it, "the fundamental rule of social intercourse under Socialism."

Socialist morality sharply condemns the exploitation of man by man and all the relations that have their origin in the exploitation practised in capitalist society. The slightest attempt to shirk one's duty to work, to live at the expense of others, to make other people work for you, is severely condemned by socialist society.

Socialist society demands of its members that in their whole conduct they be governed above all by the interests of society, of the state. A Soviet citizen draws no dividing line between his private life, his personal interests, and the paramount interests of his country. We have nothing but condemnation and contempt for that residue of the old world, for those monstrous misfits in the Soviet family, who shut themselves up in the tight shell of their personal selfish interests and are concerned only about their own welfare. Socialist society demands that people render fraternal aid to each other, demands fraternal relations with the working people of all nations and races that make up the Soviet family of peoples, demands a comradely attitude toward women as equal members of society, solicitous care of children and the aged, demands that man's dignity, his sense of honour and fairness be respected.

These principles which our socialist society enjoins upon its members find expression in such rules of social intercourse in socialist society as, for instance, "one for all, and all for one."

To the socially-minded Soviet citizen the rules of social intercourse under Socialism incorporated in the Stalin Constitution and Soviet legislation have become inner, moral needs which he is impelled to satisfy of his own volition. But in the minds of the backward section of the Soviet citizenry remnants of the old morality still survive. The new, socialist rules of social intercourse are to them only external stimuli prompting their conduct (fear of punishment, of public condemnation).

Sometimes socialist morality clashes in our country with vestiges of the old, bourgeois morality. Take the following instance to illustrate this point. Evstigney Pervoi, famous bricklayer, learnt that at the house of Morozova, whose husband was on active service, the stove was falling apart. One Saturday after work he took his tools and proceeded to her little house.

"Be a good fellow and fix my stove, won't you," she asked him.

"That's the very reason I've come," Pervoi said with a smile.

In the evening a private stove mender, with whom the mistress of the house had been negotiating, arrived on the scene. He was offended at the idea that Pervoi was doing him out of a job, as he thought, and asked:

"You must have soaked her 500 rubles, didn't you now?"

Pervoi only laughed.

When the stove was ready, Morozova asked how much she owed him for the job.

"Nothing at all," Pervoi answered.

And dozens of others in the same city have followed his example.

Socialist morality demands that all members of Soviet society build up their relations with each other on the basis of mutual comradely assistance. We highly esteem the readiness of Soviet citizens to make any sacrifice for the public good, their heroism and selfless devotion to their Soviet homeland.

The high moral qualities of the people of the Soviet Union were particularly manifest during the Great Patriotic War. The Soviet Army was victorious not only because of its proficiency in the art of war, the great generalship of its military leaders and its superiority of equipment, but also because of the incomparable moral superiority of the Soviet fighters, of the Soviet people, over the German fascist marauders.

Inculcating among the broadest strata of the population respect for the rules of social intercourse characteristic of Socialism, making the habitual observance of these rules part and parcel of their everyday life, and fostering in all members of socialist society the high moral qualities of its foremost members—constitutes one of the most important tasks confronting our Party and Young Communist League organizations.

TO SAFEGUARD AND FORTIFY PUBLIC, SOCIALIST PROPERTY

In tsarist Russia, one could hear of public, socialist property only from the lips of Bolshevik propagandists at underground meetings.

Capitalists, landlords, kulaks and bourgeois writers constantly sang the praises of private property. They sought to make the workers and peasants believe that private ownership was the alpha and omega of earthly happiness. Work by the sweat of your brow, they preached, be thrifty, remember that a penny saved is a penny earned and a prosperous and happy life will be vouchsafed to you and your children.

But this was sheer humbug.

Ask the old workers what private property meant to them. They will tell you that they never owned anything except the hands they worked with and their scanty household goods, and that the much-vaunted private property meant to them nothing but the unbridled robbery of the fruits of their labour by the capitalists.

Ask the old peasants and they will recall how muzhiks used to be beaten, flogged, haled into court and thrown into jail if their cattle trespassed on the landlord's land or if they cut some timber, hunted or collected berries in his forest. They will remember the levies made on their few possessions, how the bailiffs used to drive off the last sheep or goat for a debt owed to the landlord or the kulak, how the muzhik would be left without a shirt on his back.

And what law, pray, allowed them to do this? Again, the much-vaunted law of private property!

That was the aspect of "sacred, inviolable" private property the workers and peasants got to see. Inviolability applied only to the possessions of the propertied class. Like watchdogs the policemen, constables, police chiefs and magistrates kept vigil over the property of the capitalists, landlords and kulaks. Safeguarding private property meant to all intents and purposes safeguarding their wealth, protecting them in their "right" to rob the poor.

The power and authority of the landlords and capitalists reposed on private property, and the private ownership of the means of production was the basis upon which the entire capitalist system with its robbery and tyranny over the labouring masses was built.

All this was changed from the root up when the rule of the bourgeoisie in our country was overthrown and public, socialist ownership of the instruments and means of production was established in our entire national economy.

The factory, mill, collective farm, state farm or institution where you work, with which your entire well-being is bound up, are public property. The stores in which you buy the goods you need and the goods themselves are public property. The railways, steamships and aeroplanes that convey us from one end of the country to the other are public property. The hospital, clinic, dispensary and sanatorium where you get your medical treatment, the schools and colleges where you and your children are being taught and the theatre and cinema you visit for entertainment are all public property.

Every man of toil is vitally interested in safeguarding, fortifying and augmenting socialist property as the sacred and inviolable basis of the Soviet system, as the source of the wealth and power of our country, as the source of the life of security and culture of all our working people.

And this is a duty which the Stalin Constitution imposes upon every citizen of the Soviet Union.

Our Constitution has declared persons who commit offences against public, socialist property to be *enemies of the people.* Under Soviet law the theft of public property is most severely punished.

Public-minded Soviet citizens display the greatest solicitude and concern for the property of the people. Take the case of foreman Dolgunov, as described by the writer U. Nagibin.

Dolgunov returned from the front almost an invalid but went back to his factory, the place he was so fond of, as soon as the Germans had been driven out. Black scales encrusted the metal installations and rust had spread all over the machine tools. . . . Dolgunov touched their cold bodies with his hands. He had always treated them as if they were living beings. And now it seemed to him that the machines had merely fallen asleep, that they were bound to wake up as soon as skilled and sympathetic hands touched them. . . .

A young lad whistling a tune entered the shop. He noticed a transmission belt dangling from a smashed wheel. Without giving it much thought, he fetched a knife and cut off a length.

"Stop!" he suddenly heard someone shout from the interior of the shop.

The lad trembled and didn't dare to move an eyelash as he saw Dolgunov approaching. The latter gave him a piercing look.

"So," he said in a low voice, restraining his anger.

"What were you shouting about?" the young chap asked, blushing, "surely not about this bit of leather? Why, it would have rotted here anyhow."

"If you had been in my outfit I'd have given it to you good and proper for this bit of leather. Here every bolt and nut deserves a prayer; people gave their lives for this!"

"Who are you anyway?" the lad flung at him, now angry with shame.

"Silence!" Dolgunov rasped out, not recognizing his own voice. "Attention!"

Frightened, the lad cast a glance at him and stiffened. The piece of leather was scorching his fingers.

"I'm the boss of this place, that's who I am!" said Dolgunov in calm and impressive accents.

Every Soviet citizen should thus feel himself the owner of public property.

Concern for the preservation of public property should not be confined to protecting it from thieves and wreckers.

To safeguard and fortify public, socialist property means to fight energetically against mismanagement, extravagance, pilferage and negligence with regard to public property; it means fighting against handling it with criminal carelessness.

To safeguard and fortify public, socialist property means

managing state, co-operative and collective-farm enterprises economically, assiduously, keeping strict and audited account of public property, of the distribution of socially-owned consumer goods, and of all public money, every kopek of it.

To safeguard and fortify public, socialist property means to steadily increase the productivity of labour, to lower production costs and improve the quality of output, to extend and augment our socialist economy.

Look carefully about you; watch how your comrades at work handle the machinery, the tools, the raw materials, the fuel, the finished products; how they reap and keep the harvest in your collective farm, how the accounting and control system works, and you will find a hundred instances where public property could be better safeguarded and fortified, and a hundred ways and means of doing so.

Remember always and everywhere that public, socialist property is the foundation of our entire system, the basis of the might of our Soviet country and of our national welfare.

AN HONOURABLE DUTY OF SOVIET CITIZENS

We know from the history of our country that the Soviet government, literally on the morrow of its establishment, submitted to all governments and peoples then at war a proposal immediately to commence negotiations for the conclusion of a just and democratic peace. A decree on peace was adopted by the Second Congress of Soviets on October 26 (November 8, new style), 1917. The Soviet government has always been an ardent and determined advocate of peace and friendship among nations.

But Soviet history also tells us that the young Republic of Soviets from the very first days of its existence had to wage a severe armed struggle against foreign invaders and domestic counter-revolutionaries. V. I. Lenin said:

"In order to defend the power of the workers and peasants from the marauders, that is, from the landlords and capitalists, we need a powerful Red Army."

And such an army was created. Its organizers and leaders were V. I. Lenin and J. V. Stalin. They fostered and cherished the Soviet Army as one would a favourite child.

The Soviet Army was born and became steeled on the battlefield, in the fire of battle against the enemies of Soviet power. In 1918-20, by strenuous and glorious struggle against the enemies of the workers' and peasants' state, the Soviet Army, with the solid support of the Soviet people, successfully defended the achievements of the Great October Socialist Revolution. Had there been no Soviet Army, there would be no free and independent Union of Soviet Socialist Republics.

In 1941-45, the Soviet Army maintained the freedom and independence of the Soviet Union in a struggle of unparalleled heroism against Nazi Germany and its accomplices. The armed forces of fascist Germany and its satellites were defeated primarily and chiefly by the Soviet Army. It was the Soviet Army that took Berlin, the German capital, by storm and compelled fascist Germany to lay down its arms. The robber Nazi state, which had drenched Europe in blood, was destroyed. The Soviet Army rid our country of the constant danger of German invasion from the West.

Thereafter, the Soviet Army's determined and skilled operations in the Far East brought Japan, the last of the aggressor powers to continue the war and Nazi Germany's principal ally, to its knees. Thus the Soviet Army facilitated the speediest completion of the Second World War by the complete victory of the democratic countries. The Soviet Army rid our country of the constant danger of Japanese invasion from the East.

The Soviet Army not only freed the country from foreign invaders. It also accomplished with great credit the noble task of liberating, and of assisting in the liberation of, the peoples of Western Europe which had been trodden underfoot by the Nazi jackboot. The Soviet Army brought freedom to those who had been incarcerated in fascist prisons and concentration camps, to those who had been driven into servitude in Germany, to those who in their own countries had become the slaves of the fascist conquerors. The Soviet Army freed tens of millions in Eastern and Central Asia from enslavement at the hands of the Japanese invaders.

There is a fundamental difference between the Soviet Army and the armies of all capitalist countries.

The first and most important distinguishing feature of our army is that it was established by a country where the workers and peasants, freed by the October Revolution from capitalist oppression, hold political power, and that it serves the interests of the Soviet state. It stands guard over all the achievements of the Soviet people. It defends our land, our factories and mills, our collective and state farms, our schools and universities, our cultural treasures, our freedom and independence, our Soviet socialist country, from attack by the enemies of Soviet power.

This explains why our people feel such love for their army, are so solicitous about its welfare and are so proud of it. In our country army and people constitute a single and indivisible whole. And this is a source of strength of the Soviet Army.

The second fundamental distinguishing feature of our army is the fact that it is the army of emancipation of the formerly oppressed peoples of our country, the army which defends the national Soviet Republics, the army of friendship between the peoples of the Soviet Union. Men and commanders belonging to all the nationalities of our country serve in the Soviet Army. It is their hearth and home.

This accounts for the fact that the Soviet Army has the warm and solid support of all nationalities inhabiting our vast country. And this is another source of strength of the Soviet Army.

The third fundamental distinguishing feature of the Soviet Army is the fact that it is trained in a spirit of respect for other peoples, that it is an army that defends the right of each people to be free and independent, an army that upholds peace and friendship among the peoples of all countries.

This explains why the Soviet Army has the sympathy and support of all freedom-loving peoples in the world.

Our Constitution calls military service in the armed forces of the Soviet Union *an honourable duty of Soviet citizens*. And indeed, what duty can be more honourable than to defend with arms in hand our great Soviet country, the first socialist state of workers and peasants in the world, the hope, the bulwark of toiling humanity everywhere on the globe in its struggle for emancipation?

The armed forces of the U.S.S.R. are organized in accordance with the *universal military service law* adopted on September 1, 1939. All male Soviet citizens without distinction of nationality, race, religion, education, social origin and status must serve in the armed forces of the Soviet Union. They are called up for service at the age of 19, or 18 for those who have completed their secondary education. The period of active service is fixed at two to four years, depending upon the arm of the service. Those who have completed their active service are placed in the reserve until they are 50 years of age.

The Ministry of the Armed Forces of the U.S.S.R. is authorized to enrol and accept, and in wartime to call up for auxiliary and special service, women who have received a medical, veterinarian or special technical training.

Besides the training in the Soviet Army and Navy, elementary and pre-service military training is given in the schools and higher educational institutions.

For the training of Soviet Army commanders a large network of military schools and colleges, post-graduate courses and military academies has been instituted. The Soviet Army commanders and the rank and file are drawn from identical groups of the population, namely, the workers, peasants and intellectuals. In the Soviet Army there neither is nor can be the class antagonism that separates officers and soldiers in the armies of the capitalist countries. In the Soviet Army, officers and men constitute *one single fighting fraternity*, welded together not only by strict military discipline, but also by a profound inner moral and political unity, a unity of views, aims and aspirations, and by their utter devotion to their Soviet motherland.

The Soviet Army has adopted all the fine military traditions of the old Russian army, which creditably acquitted itself of its task of defending the country and defeating its foes. The Soviet Army has imbibed the fiery enthusiasm, the unexampled self-sacrifice and unparalleled heroism of those who fought in the greatest of all revolutions, the October Socialist Revolution.

Guided by the genius of Comrade Stalin, the Soviet Army forged its superb fighting qualities, mastered its incomparable art of defeating the enemy.

The Soviet Army is headed by talented commanders who have been trained by Comrade Stalin and are guided in their operations by the advanced military science elaborated by him.

THE SACRED DUTY OF EVERY SOVIET CITIZEN

Here is the account given by a woman Stakhanovite named A. Kirpichova, employed at one of Moscow's factories, of how she heard Comrade Stalin speak over the radio on July 3, 1941:

"As I listened to his address, I was constantly nodding my head as if saying 'yes' to every one of his words. How my heart was pounding with excitement! What had been and what was going on then flashed through my mind. I listened and heard Comrade Stalin talk about production and that we would surely smash the Germans if we worked with might and main to increase the output of tanks in our country, the output of anti-tank rifles, of aeroplanes, hand grenades and trench mortars. That's where I came in. I thought of my factory, my drilling lathe, of how many drills I spoiled until I learnt my job. But now I am happy. I've begun to turn out two quotas a day.

"When Comrade Stalin finished his speech, I walked out into the street. Moscow was blacked out and silent, but my heart was aflame, as if lightning flashed within. I kept thinking of how many parts I would be able to turn out that night. Comrade Stalin must be answered by deeds.... I stepped up to my bench and started to work. Every little screw and nut will help to save our country, I thought. And my hands, they'll turn out as much work as is needed. And not only I, but all of us in the shop worked that way."

These words of an ordinary working woman graphically express the conviction that not only the members of the Soviet Army, but *every Soviet citizen* can and must do his bit in defence of the Soviet motherland. The Stalin Constitution records this idea in the following words:

"To defend the country is the sacred duty of every citizen of the U.S.S.R."

The Constitution declares that treason to our Soviet motherland is the most heinous of crimes. The Soviet people hate and despise traitors. For treason to the socialist motherland the Soviet law exacts the severest penalty (in wartime-- shooting).

What is comprised in this sacred duty that devolves upon each citizen to defend his Soviet motherland?

This question was answered by Comrade Stalin in his well-known radio address to the people delivered on July 3, 1941. He unfolded before us a complete program of struggle in defence of our Soviet country. He said that not only the men and commanders of the Soviet Army and Navy, but all citizens of the Soviet Union must defend every inch of Soviet soil, must fight to the last drop of blood for our towns and villages. He appealed to the whole people to render all-round assistance to the Soviet Army in its struggle with the enemy. He called upon them to light the flames of partisan warfare in the enemy's rear.

If you give this Stalinist program of struggle a second thought you will see that every Soviet citizen, no matter where he might be or whatever the work engaged in, could and did readily find a groove into which he fitted. Comrade Stalin, our great leader, inspired and organized the whole Soviet people to wage a determined, heroic struggle against the insolent, despicable foe, a struggle which ended in the complete defeat of fascist Germany.

Why did the Soviet people respond so eagerly and unanimously to their leader's call, why did they fight, and fight to a finish, with such selfless devotion, with such disregard of sacrifice, until the Soviet Union had achieved complete victory?

In former times, too, the Russian people, together with other peoples of our country, fought valiantly against foreign invaders, and defeated them. But now that Soviet rule has been established in our country, the defence of the motherland has acquired special significance for the popular masses, has become a matter of paramount importance to them.

In 1918-20, the masses of the people for the first time in history were fighting in defence not only of their native country but of their own political power, for a system of government which they themselves had just set up in their native land. They were defending the land which they had drenched with their own sweat and blood, land which they had only just taken away from the landlords; they were engaged in a war for their own factories and mills which they had only just wrested from the capitalists. They were risking their lives for a country that now was *truly* their *motherland,* a *Soviet country,* which they had only just established and of which they had only just become the unrestricted masters.

That explains why our country, weak, exhausted and ill-armed at the time, was able to cope with all its numerous and powerful enemies. It was then that Lenin said: no one can ever defeat a people the majority of which has realized and come to feel that it is defending its own rule, Soviet rule, that it is fighting for a cause which ensures it and its children the opportunity of enjoying the full fruits of its labour, of receiving the full benefit of culture.

After an interval of some twenty years, the Soviet people was again compelled to engage in heroic combat against the foreign invader, to defend its political power, its country, its genuine, Soviet motherland. This time the Soviet people had already tasted free life under its new, Soviet socialist system; this time it was fighting with complete unity in its ranks not only for the opportunity of enjoying the full fruits of its labour and the full benefits of culture, but also for the already existing great blessings of free and organized labour which it itself had brought into existence.

Now less than ever before will anyone succeed in defeating such a people!

Soviet patriotism is a singular force, the like of which no other country possesses.

Every member of the Soviet community—whether he is a Russian, a Byelorussian, an Estonian, a Turkmen or a Bashkir—has a home, a land where he was born and raised. It is but natural that his thoughts and emotions should first concern his homeland and that he should dearly love it, its scenery, its people, language and culture and its glorious traditions.

He will have heard or will know from personal experience how the former rulers of this country—the tsar, the landlords and the capitalists—oppressed the people, lowered its national dignity, hated and suppressed all genuinely patriotic popular movements, kowtowed to everything foreign, and did not hesitate to betray and sell their native land to foreigners.

So much the stronger is the love and devotion which Soviet man feels for his free and independent, his happy Soviet homeland!

While each separate Soviet nation has its own home, jointly they have their one *Great Soviet Motherland*, which unites all the Soviet countries into one mighty state, the Union of Soviet Socialist Republics. The ideas and aspirations most deeply cherished by each Soviet people are inseparably bound up with this common motherland. During the war the Tajik people, for instance, addressed the following message to their sons at the front:

"When we speak of our native land, we have not only visions of the fertile valleys of the Vakhsh, the apricot and apple orchards of Leninabad or the snowcapped peaks of the

Pamirs. Our native land comprises also the green forests and deep rivers of Russia, the fertile fields of the Ukraine, the picturesque shores of the Black Sea, the mountains of the Caucasus famed in folklore and the great city of Lenin, the cradle of the revolution.

"In the centre of our mighty motherland we behold majestic Moscow, seething with activity, the heart of the country, with its ruby stars glowing on the Kremlin towers like beacons showing all the peoples of our native land the road to happiness."

The thoughts and emotions of all Soviet people have always been and continue to be addressed to their great motherland, to the Soviet Union.

Soviet citizens are immensely proud of their socialist motherland, of their social and state system which destroyed exploitation and national oppression, which established relations of co-operation and mutual assistance between people and saved the country from enthralment to foreign invaders. Soviet citizens loathe the capitalist system of exploitation with all its despicable practices, and are ready to defend their Soviet socialist country until their dying breath.

In the U.S.S.R. the social ties that bind the people together are strong and comprehensive, more so than in any other country.

The members of socialist society—the workers, peasants and the intelligentsia—are at one in interests and aspirations, in their ideas and sentiments. This unity, this feeling which imbues every Soviet citizen of being linked by indissoluble fraternal bonds with society as a whole, is one of the distinguishing features of Soviet patriotism. During the Patriotic War it was manifested daily and hourly in the active and manifold assistance rendered by the Soviet people to the Soviet Army and state.

The lofty, noble aims of this war, the profound conviction that their just cause would triumph, inspired both men and commanders of the Soviet Army and all Soviet citizens to deeds of valour and selfless labour exploits.

The Soviet people hate the enemies of the Soviet Union from the bottom of their hearts. There is a close nexus between this feeling of holy hatred and their ardent love of country.

However, national and race hatred, which debase the dignity of man, are repugnant to the Soviet character. The Soviet people fully respect the rights of other peoples. They desire to live in peace and friendship with all other peoples.

To quote Comrade Stalin:

"The strength of Soviet patriotism lies in the fact that it is based not on racial or nationalistic prejudices, but upon the profound devotion and loyalty of the people to their Soviet motherland, on the fraternal co-operation of the working people of all the nations inhabiting our country. Soviet patriotism is a harmonious blend of the national traditions of the peoples and the common vital interests of all the working people of the Soviet Union. Soviet patriotism does not disunite but unites all the nations and nationalities inhabiting our country in a single fraternal family."

Soviet patriotism multiplies the strength of our people tenfold when fighting an enemy, overcomes all difficulties, breaks down all barriers. Soviet patriotism is one of the principal sources of the strength and might of the Soviet Union.

CHAPTER VIII

THE LEADING AND DIRECTING FORCE OF THE SOVIET UNION

THE WORKING people of our country won their great rights and liberties, and established and consolidated the Soviet system of state and society under the leadership of the Communist Party of the Soviet Union (Bolsheviks). And it was under its leadership that the Soviet people successfully defended their freedom and independence in the most difficult of wars, the war against the fascist powers.

The working class and the whole labouring population of the Soviet Union has numerous non-Party organizations of various descriptions. Included here are the Soviets, which unite all the working people without any distinction whatever; the trade unions, which unite almost all workers and other employees of our country; the co-operative and collective-farm organizations, which comprise almost all our peasants and handicraftsmen; the Young Communist League of the Soviet Union, which is closely associated with the Party and contains in its ranks the advanced section of the youth of town and country; also the multifarious scientific, defence, sports and other societies, whose aggregate membership totals tens of millions.

Each one of these organizations functions in its own sphere, carries on its work independently. They all serve the interests of the people. But the Communist Party is the leading organization of the working class, of all the toiling masses, which ensures the smooth working of all non-Party organizations in one general direction; it supplies single leadership to all these organizations.

How and why has the Party been able to occupy a position of leadership among all other organizations of the working people?

The popular masses saw how over a period of many years the Bolsheviks always came out bravely and resolutely in defence of the workers and peasants, and fought against the enemies of the people of every hue and colour. The Bolsheviks exposed to the people the counter-revolutionary designs of the parties of the landlords and capitalists, revealed the antipopular policy of the tsarist regime and the bourgeois Provisional Government. The Bolsheviks waged a ruthless struggle also against the false "friends of the people," who called themselves "Socialists" but in actual practice upheld the cause of the landlords and capitalists.

The workers and peasants learnt by the experience of three revolutions what the bourgeois and pseudo-socialist parties wanted and what the Bolshevik Party was fighting for. They saw that only the Party of the Bolsheviks strove for and gained freedom and power for the working masses, happiness for the people. All other parties discredited themselves in the eyes of the people and disappeared from the scene together with the classes whose interests they had been defending.

This explains why the Communists became the sole party trusted by the popular masses.

The Party unites the foremost members of the working class, the peasantry and the intelligentsia. These people are closely connected with all non-Party organizations and as a rule head these organizations.

The Party in no way supplants any one of the non-Party organizations. The Party organizations do not domineer over the non-Party organizations but aid them in their work. Being progressive-minded and influential, the Communists who join non-Party organizations succeed in persuading these organizations to follow the line of the Party and voluntarily accept its leadership.

Let us take the Soviets of Working People's Deputies. The Soviet people choose their Deputies from among their best citizens. When the Soviets proceed to elect their leading functionaries, the Party puts up its own candidates; and if these candidates usually are elected it is for the simple reason that they have stood the test of experience and proved their devotion to the people.

The strength of the Party lies in its advanced revolutionary theory, in *Marxism-Leninism*. This doctrine is of assistance in analyzing any situation; it helps one to understand the inner connection between current events, to discern the manner and direction in which events develop, and the manner and direction of their development in the future. This doctrine enables the Party to foresee and, consequently, to direct the course of events as the interests of the popular masses, of the Soviet state, may require.

The strength of the Party lies in its being *organized*. V. I. Lenin and J. V. Stalin attach immense importance to the organization of the masses. Lenin wrote that the strength of a hundred may exceed the strength of a thousand if the hundred are organized. Owing to the organization of its ranks the Bolshevik Party has stood many a crucial test in the course of the struggle with the enemies of the people, and has successfully coped with the enormously difficult task of leading the popular masses and the Soviet state in war as well as in peace.

The strength of the Party lies in its *unity* and *discipline*, based upon unanimity of views among its members. The

Bolshevik Party demands of all its members the strictest discipline, that is, demands that Party decisions be carried out unconditionally, precisely and punctually. This Bolshevik discipline rests on the voluntary subordination of the Communists to their Party, on their wholehearted devotion to its cause.

The Party demands that every one of its members set an example, be a model worker on the job, know the technique of his trade or profession, excel in the improvement of his qualifications, in the acquisition of knowledge, in the observance of labour discipline and in compliance with the laws of the state—demands that his entire conduct in public and in private be exemplary.

The strength and invincibility of the Bolshevik Party lies in its *constant contact with the masses*. Lenin and Stalin teach that a party which has lost or even only weakened its contact with the masses loses their confidence and support and is bound to go under.

Communists never forget these words of their great leaders. They work right in the midst of the popular masses. They know what the people are interested in and strive for. Workers, collective farmers and members of the intelligentsia go to the Bolsheviks with their problems, their complaints and their proposals. The Communists do not fence themselves off from non-Party people, do not flaunt their Party membership, but give ear to the voice of the non-Party people. The Party organizations invite non-Party people to attend their open Party meetings. The Party can call upon millions of them to assist it. The Communists not only teach them but also learn from them, enrich their own experience with that of the working class, of all the toiling masses.

The Party is exceedingly solicitous of the interests and needs of the working people. It wages a ceaseless struggle to raise the material and cultural standards of the people, to strengthen the might of the Soviet Union and its international influence, to secure stable and lasting peace among the nations. The policy pursued by the Party is appreciated and understood by the popular masses; it is the life-spring of the Soviet social and state system.

That is why the Soviet people have such complete confidence in the Party of Lenin and Stalin, why they cherish it as their own Party.

The leading position of the Communist Party in the Soviet Union is emphasized and recorded in the Constitution of the U.S.S.R., which states that the Party "is the vanguard of the working people in their struggle to strengthen and develop the socialist system." The Constitution records that the Party "is the leading core of all organizations of the working people, both public and state."

Comrade Stalin called the Communist Party the leading and directing force, the force that inspired and organized the Soviet people both during the years of peaceful construction and during the years of war.

The Communist Party is one of the principal sources of the strength and might of the Soviet Union. The Soviet people owe to the Communist Party the rise and full development in our country of all other sources of the strength and might of the Soviet Union: socialist, planned economy, the moral and political unity of Soviet society, the Soviet system of state, amity among our peoples, Soviet patriotism.

The Communist Party has done and continues to carry on enormous work among the popular masses, work which has deeply penetrated their minds. It is imbuing them with the ideas of Marx, Engels, Lenin and Stalin, with the spirit of Communism.

Not so long ago Communism was merely an abstract theory.

Today Communism has become a practical aim, the rallying point of all advanced people of the Soviet Union—workers, peasants and intellectuals.

The task of giving a Communist training to the popular masses was one of the most important and urgent tasks posed at the Eighteenth Party Congress held in 1939. The Congress pointed out at the time that our country was entering the period of the completion of the building of socialist society and of a gradual transition from Socialism to Communism. This is the reason why today Communist training is of decisive importance for our country's entire future.

The most important element in Communist training is the dissemination of the theory of Marxism-Leninism among the masses. This theory contains the experience of the labour movement and of the revolutions of all countries in scientifically generalized form. This theory, as Lenin wrote, helps us "to understand more clearly the aims of its [the proletariat's] struggle, to march more firmly along the path already marked out, more confidently and firmly to seize the victory and to consolidate the victory." Soviet people cannot confine themselves to their practical work, cannot fail to concern themselves with theory. "... Practice gropes in the dark," said Comrade Stalin, "if its path is not illumined by revolutionary theory." A Soviet citizen cannot be a fully conscious and active participant in the great historical events of our era unless he masters the foundations of Marxism-Leninism.

The Communist Party sets itself the further task of constantly acquainting the masses with the policy of the Party and the Soviet state in all its different phases, so that the masses may be well informed and fully understand the reasons why this or that decision is taken and why this or that task assigned by the state must be carried out without fail by all citizens. The Communist Party aims to educate all

Soviet citizens to be ardent patriots wholeheartedly devoted to their Soviet socialist homeland and to the cause of Communism.

The Party inseparably links up Communist training with the struggle to overcome the survivals of capitalism in Soviet people's minds.

The old political and social system that existed in our country has been completely smashed and destroyed. But old people with old views, habits and customs acquired under capitalism still remain. And the old never departs, never yields to the new, without a stubborn struggle. We are all free citizens of the Soviet socialist state, members of socialist society. But this does not mean by far that all workers, peasants and intellectuals have already become advanced citizens, advanced members of our society. Comrade M. I. Kalinin said in 1944:

"There are fine, very fine people in our country, but there are also bad people.... It is only twenty-six years since our people emerged from the capitalist system and traces of the old are still left."

We still have workers, peasants and intellectuals who are concerned solely with their own personal affairs, their own narrow selfish interests. There are members of the intelligentsia who suffer from the disease that afflicted the bourgeois intellectuals of the old Russia—deference to everything foreign, oblivion to the interests of their own country.

The roots of these survivals in the mentality of Soviet people will be found not only in the past of our country but also in the influence of the capitalist countries, which trickles into the Soviet Union by devious paths.

The task of Communist training consists in making all

Soviet citizens responsible members of socialist society, conscious and active builders of Communism.

Under the leadership of the Communist Party the Soviet people are marching onward to new achievements in consolidating the might of the Soviet state, completing the building of Socialism and effecting a gradual transition to Communism.

Let us rally still more closely round the Soviet state, round the Communist Party, round our leader, friend and teacher, Comrade Stalin!

41424

ST. MARY'S COLLEGE OF MARYLAND
ST. MARY'S CITY, MARYLAND